CHECK YOUR MORALITY

KNOFEL STATON

STANDARD PUBLISHING
Cincinnati, Ohio   39971

DEDICATION

To those special people who demonstrated Christlikeness by forgiving me.

IN APPRECIATION

To Linda Merold for typing the manuscript, to Julia Staton for editing, and to Marilyn Brown for doing the final proof-reading.

Unless otherwise noted, Scripture quotations are from the New American Standard Bible, © The Lockman Foundation 1960, 1962, 1963, 1968, 1971, 1972, 1973, 1975, 1977. Quotations marked NIV are from the New International Version, © 1978 by the New York International Bible Society. Used by permission.

The "Twelve Steps" on pages 116, 117 is from *Alcoholics Anonymous,* copyright © 1939, by Alcoholic Anonymous World Services, Inc. Reprinted by permission of Alcoholics Anonymous World Services, Inc.

Library of Congress Cataloging in Publication Data:

Staton, Knofel
  Check your morality.

  1. Christian ethics. I. Title
BJ1251.S8134   1983   241   83-418
ISBN 0-87239-630-4

Sharing the thoughts of his own heart, the author may express views that are not entirely consistent with those of the publisher.

TABLE OF CONTENTS

PREFACE 5

1. TIME MARCHES ON 9

2. ABORTION 18

3. HOMOSEXUALITY 31

4. CONTRACEPTION 44

5. THE DATING GAME & TEENAGE SEX 56

6. INCEST AND PORNOGRAPHY 68

7. WHAT GOD WANTS FOR MARRIAGE 79

8. WHAT THE BIBLE TEACHES ABOUT DIVORCE 88

9. THE CHURCH AND DIVORCE 101

10. ALCOHOL 109

11. AN ETHICAL SMORGASBORD 120

12. ONCE IN SIN ALWAYS IN SIN? 129

13. HEALING THE LAND 139

At the end of each chapter are some questions **"for your**

consideration or discussion." These were written by **Dr. Bruce Parmenter** to aid you in grasping the Biblical principles involved. If you are studying this book with a group, discuss the questions within the group. If you are studying the book individually, give careful consideration to each and write your answers. Better yet, have someone else also read it and discuss the questions with you, or discuss them with someone in your family, an elder, or your minister. The more you consider these questions and verbalize your thoughts, the more you will learn to "check your morality."

FREEDOM AND MORALITY

Morality in the United States is being challenged today by many sources. One of the strongest challenges is coming from those voices that claim immorality should be allowed in the name of freedom.

Freedom is an important goal for use as individuals and as a nation. People will do a lot for "freedom." Nations go to war in order to get or keep political freedom. Children run away from home in search of their idea of freedom. Married couples divorce to participate in their definition of freedom. Some people move to the city for anonymity—another idea of freedom. Others move to the country to fewer pressures and to more flexible schedules—another concept of freedom. Others live morally reckless lives to express their idea of freedom.

Some maintain that freedom means the elimination of all absolutes ("thou shalts" and "thou shalt nots") for any absolute restrains freedom. However, the only way our freedom can be perpetuated and protected is by the acknowledgment of absolutes—the absolutes communicated to us by our Creator. *Do unto others as you would have them do unto you. Love God and others as you love yourself. "Do nothing from selfishness or empty conceit." "Do not turn your freedom into an opportunity for the flesh, but through love serve one another."* In addition to those absolute principles are some absolute practices that God commands we do or do not do.

When God says something is morally wrong, it is wrong regardless of how many people, courts, and countries say it is OK. When God says something is morally required, it must be done regardless of how many disapprove it. But those "absolutes" of God can easily become open-ended when society disregards them in practice. When society is stripped of absolutes, freedom is then available only for the person or country that has the most power. It belongs to the ones who can plan the next coup.

When the curbs that keep freedom in check are gone, each individual becomes his own authority and "life, liberty, and the pursuit of happiness" belong to the survival of the fittest. The survival of the fittest is not really survival at all. It is extinction, for someone is always destroyed in that rat race.

Real liberty means we are free to be and to act in accordance with our created nature—human beings created in the image of God. A dog is not free if it can't be and act in accordance to the nature of a dog. And a human is not free when he cannot be and act in accordance to what it means to be human—the image of God. Consequently, God not only gives us His nature—the Holy Spirit—but also absolutes. Those absolutes square with what He himself would or would not do. Only as we have His Spirit and adopt His behavior and character are we expressing the freedom of our humanness.

When we think that liberty means license to act independently of God and all other people, irresponsibility sets in and we start acting more like animals than humans—and we destroy ourselves and those around us—slowly but surely. Much of the contemporary loosening of morals is doing that to us today—all in the name of freedom.

In the name of freedom, we have pushed such things as abortion, homosexuality, and incest; and we have highlighted irresponsible thinking and action. For instance, to teach that pornography should be openly displayed and sold because some have a right to a profit is irresponsible. To saturate television programs with individual terrorism in the name of freedom of speech so that the average viewer has watched 18,000 different murders by the time he reaches his eighteenth birthday is irresponsible. For network chiefs to disregard any responsibility with the cliche "turn the knob" when they know that thousands of young children are home without parents is irresponsible.

Jesus Christ came that we may have freedom—real freedom. "It was for freedom that Christ set us free; therefore, keep standing firm and do not be subject again to a yoke of slavery" (Galatians 5:1). Christ came to set us free from the liberty that detached us from God. He came to set us free *from* the slavery to sin so we could be set free *to* reach potentials God knows we can reach.

However, we are living in a morally mixed-up world. It's not easy to know what is right and what is wrong. There are too many voices calling us to follow in too many directions. In every culture, God's people must check their ethics against the teachings of God's Word. And that's what we will be doing in this book.

However, the Biblical answers will not be satisfying to everyone. For some, the Biblical teachings will be more restrictive than they anticipate. For others, the Biblical teachings will not be as restrictive as what they are practicing. It is not our role to evaluate the Bible by our positions, but rather to evaluate our positions by the Bible and then align our positions with the Bible. Unless we do that, we practice "humanism" with a Christian mask. That means we continue to be in charge while giving a passing salute to the Bible. Unless we align our lives with the teachings of the Bible, our lips may claim that God is man's Lord but our manners demonstrate that we are our own lords. Unless we align our lives with the Bible, we may claim to be God's servants but liberate ourselves from servanthood. Thus, even the Christian must ask, "Am I *too* free? Have I become so freed from studying God's Word that I am not captivated by it?"

Christians are in a real battle. The kingdom of God and the kingdom of Satan are at odds. Christian preaching and teaching are part of God's armor in the battle. Paul put it this way:

> For though we walk in the flesh, we do not war according to the flesh, for the weapons of our warfare are not of the flesh, but divinely powerful for the destruction of fortresses. We are destroying speculations and every lofty thing raised up against the knowledge of God, and we are taking every thought captive to the obedience of Christ (2 Corinthians 10:3-5).

May our thoughts become the "prisoners of war" of Christ. Then, and only then, are we really free—for real freedom is never the right to do what we please. That is imprisonment. It eventually shackles each of us to our own individual world of self-centeredness and wants. But real freedom is the liberty to do what is right. We have that freedom when we are united to God. Then we have His Spirit, who gives us His character of righteousness, and we have His instructions, which give us His standards of right and wrong conduct. That truly liberates us to be and do what God wants us to be and do.

Chapter 1

TIME MARCHES ON

For thirteen milk bottle caps and a nickel, I could go to the movies when I was a boy. My twin sister and I would walk all over the neighborhood collecting bottle caps and hoping that our parents could give us a dime for the weekend. On Saturdays, the western classic would be shown—Hopalong Cassidy, Gene Autry, Roy Rogers, the Durango Kid. On Sundays, a drama with a moral lesson to it or a musical would be shown. Along with the main movies, a couple of short entertaining features, a cartoon, previews, advertisements, a serial, and a news update were shown. I can remember the newsreel entitled "Time Marches On." Everytime "Time Marches On" began, I used to think, "Oh no, not *that* boring stuff again." Little did I know that the least boring aspect of living is found in the truth that time marches on. For as time marches on, so do technology, travel, education, communicative abilities, and ethics.

For instance, the first time I ever rode in a car that got up to 50 MPH, I was scared to death. Now, at least twice a month, I travel by air at speeds up to 500 MPH. When I was young, my mother spent all day doing the wash. Today the wash can be done while the wife is playing tennis or taking a nap, and she doesn't even need to hang the clothes on a line to dry them. I've heard some people say, "It's the same old world." But it's not. It's a different world entirely. In fact, it's so different that our great grandparents would think they had stepped onto a different planet were they to visit us today.

It's thrilling to be a part of change, but it can also be frightening. People need stability along with progress. Just a steady diet of modifications can throw us into what some have called "future shock." Where do we find stability in the midst of constant shufflings? Is there an anchor that can hold us steady instead of drifting so that we are totally dependent upon the winds for the next change of direction? Do we have a compass that can keep us going in the proper direction?

Of course, we do. The only way we can survive this constantly changing world is to be properly positioned. Notice, I did not say that we must have proper positions, but must be properly positioned. We can have "proper" positions today that become totally different "proper" positions tomorrow. Our environment has a way of making what was an improper position yesterday to become a "proper" position today. When the situations determine our ethics, there is no stability. We are totally cut loose to be tossed here and there by the waves of society.

Where is stability then? It is found in what does not change, or more accurately, in who does not change. Stability is found in God, "Who is and who was and who is to come" (Revelation 1:8). He is the Eternal One. He is the Solid Rock. People who have come through changes without losing their senses rightly looked to God as their help, refuge, strong tower, shelter, safety, rock, and fortress (Psalms 61, 62). Anchoring one's life in God is not a crutch for the psychologically immature, as some suggest. Instead, it is how the sensible ones survive—the ones who have rightly understood history and who rightly anticipate the future, the ones who refuse to keep their heads in the sand, the ones who would not say to the world, "Stop, I want to get off." The world is not going to stop until Jesus returns, and sensible people do not cry the blues or try to escape from being involved. At the same time, sensible people do not allow themselves to be captured or molded or shaped by the times. They refuse to be as dead fish that go whichever way the stream goes. Sensible people are stable people because they are positioned in God through Jesus (John 14:6). And from that position, they make stands on the ethical issues of the day.

It is what we do with the ethical issues that will make or break us in the business world, industrial world, space-age world, nuclear world, or any world. But it can also make or break us in the day-by-day activities in which each of us is involved—relationships with our friends, families, co-workers, neighbors, and even with our own bodies. When I consider what society is doing with ethical issues today, I think of a truck that has started down a steep hill with faulty brakes. As it goes faster and faster down the hill, someone piles on more weight in the bed of the truck, conjures up a 100 MPH tailwind, and pours slick oil on the highway ahead. Disaster is sure to result.

The devil is working that way with us today. He continues to pile on heavier ethical issues, while backing them up with the tailwind of peer pressure. He uses the mass media to make the issues attractive and then reduces the resistance by liberal court rulings and community acceptance.

But the truck doesn't have to crash. It can negotiate on a "runaway turn off" ramp until it comes to a gradual halt. Then new brakes can be put on. It is my hope that this book can serve as one of those runaway turn off ramps and slow down our propensity for disaster.

As time marches on, the issues are indeed getting heavier. The closest I got to pornography as a boy growing up was the women's underwear section of the Sears, Roebuck catalog. Today, by the time a child is ten, he has seen and heard it all. I'll never forget the shock I got when our son was seven years old. I took him to school with me one day and left him in my office while I took some test papers to student mailboxes. When I returned, I noticed on the cover of a religious journal on my desk a four-letter sex word clearly printed. My heart sank. Surely that didn't come from the pen of my seven-year-old. I was about to finish junior high school before I had ever heard the word. Hesitantly I asked, "Son, did you write this?"

And as proud as a peacock he replied, "Sure did, dad."

"Oh, no," I thought. "Is he going to become the porno literary king of paperbacks?" I then mustered enough nerve to ask the next question.

"Son, do you know how to pronounce it?"

Perfect enunciation! My heart sank. How can this possibly be? He's my son! He's supposed to know nothing at seven. I didn't! "Do you know what it means, son?"

"Nope. Haven't got the slightest idea."

11

Whew! Relief! "But how did you know how to pronounce it?"

"I've heard kids at school say it."

"How did you know how to spell it?"

"I've seen it on bathroom walls."

Believe me, by the time most of our kids are in the sixth grade, they know about ethical issues we didn't know existed when we were that age.

The ethical issue that was guaranteed to get us into trouble when I was in high school was whose outhouse to turn over on Halloween. And if we wanted to be really mean, we waited until someone was inside it. Every high school had its moral misfits then as well as today. The tough "hood" type of guys when I was in high school were those who occasionally would buy a six-pack, drive to the country, drink the beer, and come back to town. They were the real meanies. But today, that's Mickey-Mouse stuff. Today kids can watch the X-rated movies in their bedrooms on their own TVs; they can take a pill to get going and a pill to wind down, and a pill to hop from one bed to another; and if that doesn't work, they can abort one day and be in classes the next. If they strike out with the opposite sex, they can turn to their own sex as an "acceptable" alternative. And that is just the tip of the iceberg. Anything goes in a permissive society that has idolized the philosophy of pulling your own strings and looking out for number one. Anything that helps the individual achieve is becoming OK. The use of psychological, sociological, and physical power that hurts others but seems to benefit self is becoming acceptable in both corporate and individual ethical decisions. Sometimes success and sin seem to be synonymous.

As the "load" gets heavier and the resistance gets weaker, parents and children alike wonder whether there is help from anywhere. There is help. A lot of it. One source of powerful help is the church.

However, not just *any* church is sufficient. Churches can be as counterfeit as bogus currency. Churches that really help are people-oriented, Christ-centered, and Bible-based. That kind of church is not made up of perfect people, but forgiven people who are positioned in God through Jesus. A church that does not teach the Bible is a church that is caught in the stream without a rudder. It will simply drift with the times. In fact, it might feed more permissiveness into the stream. But a Christ-centered, Bible-based church is a real support to people who live in a permissive society. Not only does such a church share God's absolutes about what is moral and immoral, but it also teaches principles that help people make decisions about those hundreds of issues that are worldly neutral.

But the church's help does not come only from its content base, but also from its community base. People need the support of people. We need to be able to go to some people when we aren't handling things right. The church should be the people we feel we can go to.

In a Sunday school class I attended recently, one person shared that her thirteen year-old son had been caught smoking marijuana and was suspended from school. "I do not know what to do. I need help," she pleaded. Another person shared that her husband had lost his business and had started drinking. "What should I do? How can I handle this?" A couple shared that they had been separated, but were now together and needed the support of their church family. Another woman shared that she lives away from her immediate family and has no one to turn to when she's had all she can take from her kids. In fact, she confessed that her daughter had a knot on her head because she had hit her that morning.

All of these people were saying the same thing—"I need a support group of people as I walk through the pressures of the day." The church should provide that support group.

The church should also be that group of people that extends forgiveness. It is one thing to hear that God forgives, but it is another thing to experience the forgiveness of God flowing through people who are His people. That's the church. While the world around us pulls us apart—apart from God, apart from each other, and apart from ourselves—the church lives to bring reconciliation. In fact, every ethical situation that is immoral is immoral precisely because it destroys relationships. As time marches on, our relationships must not deteriorate, or we will destroy ourselves.

Maintaining right relationships is what the content of the

13

Bible is all about. That's why the helpful church is Bible-based. The Bible is our "Godufactured" guide. To go against its counsel is to go against sound wisdom.

Some people rebel against Biblical absolutes because they misunderstand the purposes of those absolutes. God is not a fuddy-duddy bore of the party who whips out a new negative command every time He notices that we are having a good time. But some people have seen Him as an eternal "Scrooge"—an eternal prison warden, keeping watch on every move we make so He can punish us when we goof it!

That's not the Creator God of the Bible. God is the God of love. He knows exactly how we tick. He knows both what harms us and what helps us. Consequently, every negative and positive command in the Bible comes out of God's care for us. I call them God's guardrails along the highway of life. He has put them there to protect us from toppling off the deep end so we do not destroy ourselves or others.

He wants us to enjoy our journey on planet earth, not begrudge it. But He wants us to behave so that other people can enjoy their journey in life also. To disregard His counsel is to head toward despair, not delight; toward fettering, not freedom; toward frustration, not fulfillment.

As many ethical issues confront us, many different voices bombard us with the decisions we ought to make. Should we abort a pregnancy, drink alcoholic beverages at a social, divorce and remarry, or live with a potential mate outside of marriage? Our contemporary culture pulls us into many different directions as we stand at the threshold of these decisions. Which way is the right way?

It is time that we turn to the One who cares about us more than anyone else and hear Him. We must turn to the Bible, which can anchor us and give us stability as the winds and the waves of the times continue to blow.

Biblical ethics does not take its clue from what our environment says is right or wrong, but from God. Biblical ethics is the conformity of human behavior to the will of God. Biblical ethics is tied up with the idea of a covenant. Covenant is not a bargain we strike up with God as if God and we are on the same level. Oh, no! We are not on the same level. God is Creator and Lord. He has initiated His covenant out of His love. He wants us to be holy as He is holy. To be holy means to be different. The primary way the godly person is different is that he lives not just for self, but also for others. In fact, the primary criterion for human behavior that squares with the will of God is this—concern for another's well being. Paul put it this way:

> Let no debt remain outstanding, except the continuing debt to love one another, for he who loves his fellow man has fulfilled the law. The commandments, 'Do not commit adultery,' 'Do not murder,' 'Do not steal,' 'Do not covet,' and whatever other commandment there may be, are summed up in this one rule: 'Love your neighbor as yourself.' Love does no harm to its neighbor. Therefore, love is the fulfillment of the law (Romans 13:8-10, NIV).

Love is the principle that undergirds every commandment of God. And it is the principle that is to undergird every behavior of God's people (1 John 2:5-11; 3:11-24; 4:11, 21). "By this we know that we love . . . when we love God and observe His commandments" (1 John 5:2).

Human behavior that squares with the will of God squares with love. Real love does no harm to God, self, or another. But here's the rub. Just what kinds of behavior do harm? God has not left us adrift in the sea of opinions about that. Any "thou shalt nots" from God give us insight about harmful behavior. Our obligation is to obey God, because we trust that He knows people better than we do. Any human voice that approves a behavior God doesn't is a voice that does not properly understand human nature. To say "this helps" a person when God condemns that behavior is to admit stupidity about humanity. After thousands of years, we are still too unlearned about human nature. That's why text books on psychology and sociology become somewhat outdated by the time they hit the bookstores. And that's why our primary source for proper and improper human behavior must come from the Bible.

If every person in our culture and every law in our country approves a behavior that God doesn't, who's right? God is! The question is, whom will we worship—God or culture? That will be partly answered by another question—whose approval do we want? We bow down to get approvals. Our egos need to be stroked by *someone*. Caving in to the world will be an ongoing temptation for the Christian. Therefore,

15

Paul wrote, "Do not be conformed to this world but be transformed by the renewing of your mind, that you may prove what the will of God is, that which is good and acceptable and perfect" (Romans 12:2). J. B. Phillips paraphrased it this way: "Don't let the world around you squeeze you into its own mold, but let God remold your minds . . ." (The New Testament in Modern English). Clarence Jordan translated it, "And don't let the present age keep you in its cocoon . . ." (The Cotton Patch Version of Paul's Epistles).

Much of what you will read in this book will go against the "squeeze" of this world. This book will not fit into the "cocoon" that has been formed over the past few decades. It will call for some radical changes.

Whether or not we decide to be different depends partly upon whether or not we will take God seriously when we read that He is both Lord and Judge. It will also depend upon whether we want to be *temporarily* stroked or stroked *forever*. Make no mistake about it—a person will get stroked by the world if he goes along with the crowd. But that will not last long.

Do not love the world or anything in the world. If anyone loves the world, the love of the Father is not in him. For everything in the world—the cravings of sinful man, the lust of his eyes and the boasting of what he has and does—comes not from the Father but from the world. The world and its desires pass away, but the man who does the will of God lives forever (1 John 2:15-17, NIV).

Yes, time marches on. But may you march beyond time—into eternity with God. "See that what you have heard from the beginning remains in you. If it does, you also will remain in the Son and in the Father. And this is what he promised us—even eternal life" (1 John 2;24, 25, NIV). "If you know that he is righteous, you know that everyone who does what is right has been born of him" (1 John 2:29, NIV).

For Your Consideration or Discussion

1. For adults: How have moral issues changed since you were a teen-ager (if you think they have).

2. What is your understanding of a "moral absolute"? What does that phrase mean?
3. What moral absolutes are found in the Bible? (Search this chapter for clues.) Can the moral absolutes of the Bible be reduced to one or two? If so, what are they?
4. Do you believe in the reality of the devil? If you do, what do you think is the relation between satanic influence and human responsibility. For example, if we are tempted by Satan or under his power, is our sinning Satan's fault or ours?
5. Consider morality in relation to the mission of the church. For example, is it the purpose of the church to foster morality or to preach grace? Are morality and redemption the same thing? Is the church primarily an ethical community or a redemptive community? Do you go to church to learn how to be moral or for some other reason? If for some other reason, what is that reason?
6. Do you agree with Mr. Staton's assertion, "Biblical ethics is the conformity of human behavior to the will of God"?

Chapter 2

ABORTION

A mini-diary:

Oct. 5 - Today my life began. My parents don't know it yet. I am as small as the seed of an apple, but I am to be a girl. I shall have blonde hair and blue eyes. Just about everything is settled, though. Even the fact that I shall love flowers.

Oct. 19 - Some say that I am not a real person yet—that only my mother exists. But my mother is, and I am.

Oct. 25 - My heart began to beat today, all by itself. From this hour on it shall gently beat for the rest of my life without ever stopping to rest. And after many years it will tire. It will stop, and then I will die.

Nov. 2 - I'm growing a bit every day. My arms and legs are beginning to take shape, but I have to wait a long time yet before these little legs will raise me to my mother's arms, before these little arms will be able to gather flowers and embrace my father.

Nov. 10 - I'm going to be pretty. My facial features are clearly formed—a cute little nose, dimples, dainty ears, and lips. I can hardly wait to place those little lips next to mother's cheek with the kiss of love—just from me.

Nov. 20 - It was just today that the doctor told Mom that I am living here under her heart. If she could just see me now. I truly look like a tiny baby already. I'm a very real little person. Oh, how happy she must be. Are you happy, Mom?

Nov. 25 - My mom and dad are probably thinking about a name for me, but they don't even know that I am a girl. They are probably saying Andy, but I want to be called Cathy.

Dec. 24. - I wonder if Mom hears the whispering of my heart. Some children come into the world sick and then the delicate hands of the doctor perform miracles to bring them to health, but my heart is strong and healthy. It beats so evenly. You'll have a healthy little daughter, Mom.

Dec. 28 - Today my mother killed me.

(Author unknown)

Is that really correct? Was there a real person inside that mother? On January 22, 1973, the Supreme Court ("Rowe vs. Wade") supposedly elevated the extermination of unborn babies to the "humane" level by legally declaring that unborn babies under six months of age are nonpersons. And as nonpersons, they would not be protected by our constitution.

If unborn babies are nonpersons, abortion is no more of a moral issue than getting rid of an unwanted bag of garbage. Both the baby and the bag are mere things! Thus, getting rid of such a baby cannot be considered murder—so said the Supreme Court.

It is interesting to note that the same Supreme Court that de-humanized unborn babies and withdrew protection from them stopped the construction of a $116 million dam in Tennessee because the life of a three-inch snail darter was endangered, and a $340 million dam in California because the life of a ⅝" long-legged spider was threatened by the dam. What a tragic course we are traveling upon when snails ans spiders have more value than unborn babies.

Not only did the Supreme Court permit abortions, but the U.S. Government decided to pay for them. By August 4, 1979, $50 million of federal funds per year were being spent to fund abortions. Federal funds were stopped on August 4, 1979, but were resumed four months later. On the day the funds were resumed, the front page of the *Joplin Globe* in Joplin, Missouri, had two major articles that were ironically placed alongside each other. One article was entitled, "Fund Abortions." The other was entitled, "Save a Dog's Life." The second article told about a woman who had requested in her will that her dog be "put to sleep." But after the woman's death, a group of lawyers teamed up to deny the request. Court battles were waged for months and resulted in the life of the dog being spared and a new law being signed by Governor Brown. The new California law prohibits any will from requesting the death of anything. However, the same year, Governor Brown's state budget included $32 million for funding abortions in that one state alone. In fact, California performs between 100-200,000 abortions every year. Wholesale abortions do not happen only in "liberal" California. In 1979, 21.8% of all pregnancies in the state of Missouri were aborted. Nearly one-third of all pregnancies are now being aborted in America.

Since 1973, we have aborted nearly twelve million unborn babies in this country alone. That's double the resulting deaths of Hitler's holocaust. But at least he went after people who could run and hide. However, there is no unborn baby who can run. His only hiding place is in the refuge of his mother's body.

Although an outcry against abortions is emerging, there are several sources that continue to feed the escalation of abortions. One national "women's rights" group has printed the following:

A woman's sexuality is severely limited by the continual fear of pregnancy. To gain control we must control reproduction functions of the body. We must have safe and effective birth control and access to free, legal, and safe abortions. The decision to have a child is ours and ours only, not the doctor's, not the father's, not anyone else's. We women are the only ones in the position to decide whether or not we can care for a child both emotionally and physically.

That kind of emotional position draws supporters. The leaders make an interesting claim: "We are not for abortion, but against mandatory motherhood." I say, "A rose by any other name smells the same."

The sex choice position is emerging. This position states that not only do women have a right to decide whether or not they want a baby, but also what kind of baby—a boy or a girl. Sophisticated tests (amniocentesis) can determine the sex of the child to be. Consequently, some are saying that the mother has a right to abort the fetus if it isn't the sex she wants. Basing a decision of abortion on sex selection may throw us into a major imbalance. Participants at the 1978 conference at the Harvard Medical School pondered the risk of male-female imbalance in the future because the majority of parents prefer a boy.

Probably the most powerful support for abortion comes from a growing philosophy of humanism and individualism, which raises the banner of "look out for number one." That philosophy can opt for abortion on such grounds as inconvenience to a career, a planned trip, or a planned purchase that might have to be deterred.

What should be the position of the church in all of this? What kind of counsel can parents give to each other and to their children? The issue centers around one question. Is the fetus a person or a thing? If it is a thing, then abortion is no more a moral issue than taking a car to the dump. But if the fetus is a person, then an abortion is taking a life of another.

If the issue centers around whether or not the fetus is a person, then we must ask, "Does the Bible give us any clues about that question?" It does.

Here are some Biblical passages that we need to consider:
1. Amos 1:13: "For three transgressions of the sons of Ammon and for four I will not revoke its punishment, because they ripped open the pregnant women of Gilead in order to enlarge their borders." In the interest of material increase, the Ammonites destroyed human increase prior to the birth of the humans. And God called that evil.
2. 2 Kings 8:12: "And Hazael said, 'Why does my lord weep?' Then he answered, 'Because I know the evil that you will do to the sons of Israel: their strongholds you will set on fire, and their young men you will kill with the sword, and their little ones you will dash in pieces, and their women with child you will rip up.' " Notice that ripping open the pregnant women is put in the same category as killing little children and young men.
3. 2 Kings 15:16-18: "Menahem struck Tiphsah . . . and he ripped up all its women who were with child" (v. 16). Menahem's was a life-style judged in these words: "He did evil in the sight of the Lord" (v. 18).

In the above cases, the lives of both the mother and the baby were endangered, and the action was done without the consent of the mother. Consequently, these cases are not the same as the scene today. However, we may be able to infer from these sections that the expectant mothers had life in them. And there is no hint about the length of the pregnancies. We do not read that the action was evil only after the third month—or fourth—or sixth. These women were not considered to be with "lifeless embryo," but were said to be "with child."

If those were the only passages we had to consider, the issue would indeed be quite unclear. But the Bible fine tunes the issue for us.

1. Job 31:15: "Did not He who made me in the womb make him, and the same one fashion us in the womb?" Notice Job said it was a "me" that was formed in the womb. He was as much Job in the womb as he was to be Job in the world.

2. Job 10:18, 19: Job asked, "Why then has Thou brought me out of the womb? Would that I had died and no one had seen me!" Job spoke about dying before birth. There can be no dying before birth unless there is living before birth. Job must have thought about life at such an early stage that when it dies no eye would see him. That's *very* early.

3. Psalm 139:13: "For Thou didst form my inward parts. Thou didst weave me in my mother's womb." The psalmist understood that he was a "me"; he was not just a mass of material that was developing.

4. Jeremiah 1:5: "Before I formed you in the womb I knew you. And before you were born I consecrated you." At the moment of conception, before any "forming" was done, God said I knew "you." Both before forming and before birth a "you" existed.

5. Genesis 25:23: "And the Lord said to her, 'Two nations are in your womb; and two peoples shall be separated from your body. . . .'" Doesn't that sound like *life?*

6. Psalm 51:5: The mother conceived a "me."

7. Genesis 30:2: "Then Jacob's anger burned against Rachel, and he said, 'Am I in the place of God, who has withheld from you the fruit of the womb?'" Fruit refers to life to be ripened.

8. Hosea 9:11: "As for Ephraim, their glory will fly away like a bird—no birth, no pregnancy, and no conception."

In this verse, we see the states of maturation: First conception, then pregnancy, then birth.

9. Exodus 21:22-25: "And if men struggle with each other and strike a woman with child so that she has a miscarriage, yet there is no further injury, he shall surely be fined as the woman's husband may demand of him; and he shall pay as the judges decide. But if there is any further injury, then you shall appoint as a penalty life for life, eye for eye, tooth for tooth, hand for hand, foot for foot, burn for burn, wound for wound, bruise for bruise."

   Some use this verse to suggest that what is in the womb is not human life; so if it were destroyed, there was no problem unless a further injury occurred—that is, to the mother. However, the text does not support that position. Here are some important points to consider: (1) The English word "miscarriage" used here is misleading. The Hebrew word for miscarriage *(shachol)* is not used here. Instead, the Hebrew words literally mean a "child goes out" *(yeled* and *yatza).* This text is describing the premature exodus of a child that was developing in the womb. The NIV rightly translates it as "gives birth prematurely." (2) The word *further* in regard to the injury, is not in the Hebrew text. Thus, the injury is not restricted just to the mother, but also the child. The point is that if people force the premature birth of a child (regardless of the length of gestation), they shall be punished according to the results. If the child dies, then capital punishment was required of the person who forced the exodus. "Life for life" makes it clear that life is in the womb.

10. Matthew 1:18: Mary "was found to be with child." Inside Mary was a *child,* not a *thing.*

11. Luke 1:15: ". . . he will be filled with the Holy Spirit, while yet in his mother's womb." Is that a nonperson?

12. Luke 1:36: "Elizabeth has also conceived a son." Notice a *son* was conceived, not a *thing* that might become a son.

13. Luke 1:44: The unborn *baby* "leaped" in the womb. Notice a "baby" leaped in the womb, not a blob.

14. Luke 1:57: "Now the time had come for Elizabeth to

give birth, and she brought forth a son." Why did Elizabeth bring forth a *son?* Because that's what was conceived. He was a son from conception.

The Bible does not make a distinction between life before birth and life after birth. The same Hebrew word in the Old Testament *(yeled)* and the same Greek word in the New Testament *(brephos)* are used to describe both the unborn and born child.

No wonder the Bible speaks about the blessing of the womb and especially of the fruit of the womb (Deuteronomy 7:13; Genesis 49:25).

We ought to be more concerned about the *life* that is in the womb. There is no biological data that suggests to us that a nonperson exists in the womb prior to a certain month determined by the courts. At the time of conception, a genetic entity begins and will never be repeated. Life develops in remarkable and predicatable ways.

Genetically, the fetus is a human life. Dr. Bernard Nathanson observes that it is from biochemistry that we know that the fetus is an entity of its own and not just a part of the mother's body. He quotes Daniel Callahan who said, "Genetically, hormonally, and in all organic respects, save the source of its nourishment, a fetus and even an embryo is separate from the woman" *(Aborting America,* pp. 203, 204). Conception produces life that has forty-six chromosomes with all the DNA (genetic code) that a fully mature adult has. Within that life is contained the color of eyes, length of nose, hair texture—all the physical features of the developing person. The embryo or fetus is life in development, and life will develop according to the instructions in the genetic code. Within fourteen days, the sex of the embryo can be verified. By day eighteen, the heart begins to beat. By day twenty, the basics of the central nervous system (brain, backbone, and spinal cord) are established. The liver, kidneys, and digestive tract are taking shape. By day thirty, the eyes, ears, and nose begin to form and the person is 10,000 times longer than at fertilization. By day thirty-one, nerve root fibers in the spinal cord are visible. By day thirty-three, the differentiation of the cerebral cortex can be detected. By day thirty-five, the color of the eyes has formed. By day thirity-six, the nervous system begins stimulating muscles.

24

By day forty-three, brain waves can be detected. By day forty-four, eyelids are formed. By day forty-five, the life responds to touch and can feel pain. By day forty-six, 600,000 ova are present in the female infant. By day fifty, the digestive juices are present and the kidneys are extracting waste. By day sixty, the person truly looks like a tiny baby. By the eleventh week, all parts are formed but still continue to develop. In fact, changes in the body will continue until death, regardless of how long the person lives. By the end of the third month, the unborn person reaches out, scratches his nose, raises his head, kicks his legs, curls his toes, moves his thumbs, makes a fist, squints, frowns, opens his mouth, sucks his thumb, sleeps and wakes, and even inhales and exhales. He actually drinks amnionic fluids and will digest and excrete the fluid.

Both the Biblical and biological data support the view that life-in-development begins at conception. Consequently, abortion is not first of all a medical issue, but a moral issue. It violates the Hippocratic Oath, the standard for Western medical ethics, which in part says, "I will not give to a woman a pessary to produce an abortion." Abortion violates the Declaration of Geneva from the World Medical Association, which states, "I will maintain the utmost respect for life from the time of conception until death." Today, many medical schools do not refer to the Hippocratic Code and have deleted "from the time of conception" from the Declaration of Geneva.

We are headed toward a self-destructive path when the legal courts can define person and nonperson—life and death. The January 22, 1973, decision of the Supreme Court removed unborn babies in the early stages of life from the protection of the fourteenth amendment—"nor shall any state deprive any person of life. . . ." The courts decided that a fetus in the early stages is not a person. The courts legally declared a fetus to be a person when it is "potentially able to live outside the mother's womb." Then one of the justices added, "Viability is usually placed at about seven months, but may occur earlier, even at 24 weeks."

It is true that the unborn baby needs the environment of his mother, but that doesn't make him any less a person than we who are born needing the environment of the earth's atmosphere for our survival. Take us out of this environment, and we will not survive long. Does that mean we are nonpersons in *this* stage of our development?

But what about all the arguments for abortion? Are they valid?

1. "The woman and her body." It is her body. A man doesn't get pregnant. However, no person has absolute use of his own body at the expense of another.
2. "Isn't a legal abortion safer than an illegal one?" This ignores the morality of the issue. Sin is often an "easy way out." Besides, for whom is it safer? Certainly not for the unborn person. Both the illegal and legal abortion have the same fatality rate for the babies. Statistics about the death rate of illegal abortions for the mother have been grossly exaggerated, according to experts. The total listed deaths due to illegal abortions the year before the Supreme Court legalized abortions was thirty-nine. Those were listed deaths, but how about those not listed as caused by illegal abortion. (Let's face it, not everyone will admit an illegal abortion.) Dr. Nathanson estimates the total deaths to be 500 (p. 193). While 500 possible deaths is high, it is certainly not as high as 4,000 certain deaths per day that now occur to unborn babies.
3. "If abortion is not legalized, the women will get them anyway." On that basis, why not eliminate all laws? Again, this argument ignores the moraltiy of the issue.
4. "We are overpopulated. We can't take care of the people we have." The world's main problem is not overpopulation, but the lack of Christian ethics to care for people. The hunger in the world is not due to too many people, but inadequate distribution. Politics causes more hunger than people. We have enough farm land between the lanes of our interstate highway system to feed several countries if we would plant, cultivate, and harvest the space. We will never solve the hunger problem in India by aborting babies in Indianapolis.
5. "Abortion is a benefit to society." Where are the benefits?
6. "It's a crime to bring unwanted babies into the world.

They will become abused children." There is no evidence that children who are abused are children who were not wanted. Child abuse seems to be more related to family history, high mobility that takes us away from support groups, and the stress on "do your own thing." Child abuse has actually increased since the legalization of abortions. When we talk about unwanted children, we need to ask, "Unwanted by whom?" There is a waiting list for adopting newborn babies. It may be tough and bring sadness to give a baby up for adoption, but it isn't a sin and shouldn't produce guilt. It's a way to preserve life—and thus to love the baby.

If the facts were known, many parents were surprised when the news broke, "You're going to have a baby." And many did not want that news. Many of us were unwanted at one time or another. I can't imagine my folks wanted a new set of twins during the Depression when they had already had three children and were in their mid-thirties. But am I glad they didn't abort me!

7. "Abortions reduce the death rate of infants." How ridiculous! It raises the death rate, for every aborted baby becomes a statistic. The fact that babies that are born have a reduced death rate today has nothing to do with abortion. That's like saying the death rate of people over fifty is reduced because we kill a million teenagers a year. We don't add to a baby's life span by killing unborn babies.

8. "Abortion encourages use of contraceptions." That hasn't been the case. In fact, it decreases the use of contraceptives.

9. "Abortion should be allowed when the life of the mother is threatened." In one sense, the life of the mother is always threatened by pregnancy. However, today it is a rarity for a mother to die during childbirth. Deciding a mother will die before the fact can never be done with certainty. But deciding that a little life will die ahead of the fact *can* be determined and executed.

10. Shouldn't pregnancy by rape dictate abortion? Preg-

nancy by rape is very rare. But what if a pregnancy does occur? That is certainly an anguishing situation for a woman to face. The rape was certainly immoral. Aborting the baby cannot *reverse* the immorality nor the trauma of the rape. As the woman does not risk her life to resist the attacker, should she take the life of another because the attack has taken place? One-half of the baby is from her—her genes and chromosomes. What a bond of love that child can have with the mother by knowing the mother did not abort a baby the mother did not plan or want.

11. Shouldn't pregnancy by incest be aborted? Incest is rising in this country. It is a terrible crime. And pregnancy as a result of incest adds to the anguish of a woman. It is probably wise to apply the same criterion for pregnancy by incest as by rape. If every pregnancy by rape and incest were aborted, some of the great contributors in our world's history would have been aborted.

To go the way of abortions for any of the above reasons is to cop out on problems rather than face them. But to cop out is not God's answer. It wasn't His answer when Jesus prayed, "If it is possible, let this cup pass from me." And it isn't His answer for us today. A pregnancy may cause suffering and some shame, but God teaches that we grow through difficulties (1 Peter 4:12-19; James 1; Romans 5:1-5).

The continuation of legalized abortions can have some of the following results:

1. The further loosening of sexual fidelity.
2. The further cheapening of human life. If an unproductive unborn baby can be eliminated for convenience sake, then why not an unproductive aged person?
3. A security threat. Could we eventually have more senior citizens than young people? If so, who would defend us in the case of national security?
4. An economic threat. How well can a decreasing youth population financially support the retirement and Social Security benefits of an increasing senior population?
5. An idiological threat. How well can a declining population base in the United States with the ideology of our

Constitution withstand the increasing population base of such ideologies as Communism?

6. The increase of infanticide. Infanticide is the killing of newborn infants. Clear evidence reveals that many abortion attempts resulted in the birth of live babies who were intentionally killed or allowed to die without any attempt to save them.

However, the above potentialities should not be the determing factor about whether or not to abort. The determining factor should rest upon the evidence that conception begins human life and the teachings of God about how we treat life.

In addition to those criteria, we should apply some additional New Testament principles to the abortion issue. These general principles are relevant:

1. The identifying mark of the Christian is love—agape style. Agape love is always unconditional love for another's well being. How can agape love be applied to a baby by abortion?
2. 2 Corinthians 5:16. We are to look at life from a different perspective. From God's perspective.
3. Romans 15:1-3. We are to make decisions to please others, not ourselves.
4. Philippians 2:4. We are not to look out for just our own personal interests, but also the interests of others. That includes the interests of unborn babies.
5. Matthew 16:24. We are to deny ourselves and take up our cross. Taking up a cross always involves the willingness to die so that another might live.
6. Romans 8:2. Christians have received the Spirit of life. How is the Holy Spirit of life expressed if we vote to kill babies?
7. 1 John 2:6. We are to walk as Jesus walked. He maintained a high value on life—especially the life of children.
8. 1 John 4:17. In everything we are to glorify or characterize God. Does abortion do that?

The only life that is created in the image of God is human life. Instead of aborting the image of God, we should adore that image. More of us should adopt the attitude of Susan Revitt of Boyville, New York, who wrote:

I always wanted a white shag rug, I thought it would look nice,
Then I had my first child. That made me think twice.
I always wanted some Lenox pieces to put on the table and
admire,
And then we had our first child and I opted for a dryer.
I always wanted glass table tops and crystal like a bell,
And then I had our first child and thought plastic would do as
well.
I always wanted so many things I always wished for,
But when I saw my first child, I wanted children so much more.

When the potential birth of a baby poses a serious difficulty, rather than abort, we should seek the support of family, friends, and God's people while remembering the words of the apostle Peter:

Humble yourselves, therefore, under the mighty hand of God, that He may exalt you at the proper time, casting all your anxiety upon Him, because He cares for you. Be of sober spirit, be on the alert. Your adversary, the devil, prowls about like a roaring lion, seeking someone to devour. But resist him, firm in your faith, knowing that the same experiences of suffering are being accomplished by your brethren who are in the world. And after you have suffered for a little while, the God of all grace, who called you to His eternal glory in Christ, will Himself perfect, confirm, strengthen and establish you. To Him be dominion forever and ever. Amen (1 Peter 5:6-11).

For Your Consideration or Discussion

1. How would you counter the position expressed in the quotation from the women's rights group found on page 20?
2. In your opinion, is a fetus a person? If it is, list the arguments found in this chapter to support that and add your own.
3. Mr. Staton states, "The embryo or fetus is life in development. . . ." Do you agree? Would you agree with this statement: "All human life is life in development"? If that is true, would you agree that destruction of any human life, without sufficient cause, is morally wrong? Or would you remove the phrase "without sufficient cause"? Discuss.

Chapter 3

HOMOSEXUALITY

Homosexuality is not a modern phenomenon. Homosexual acts are recorded in some of our oldest existing literature. Pictures of homosexual activities have been found on the walls of caves and on pieces of pottery. Biblically, we have evidences of homosexuality as early as the contemporaries of Abraham.

Today homosexuality is coming out of the closet. Some movie and television plots present homosexuality as an alternative life-style. Several magazines are marketed for the homosexual client. Books, both pro and con, are being published. Some major religious denominations ordain homosexual ministers. Known homosexuals are being appointed to such posts as state and federal judges. Some cities hire known homosexuals as policemen. Some boards of education have approved the teaching of homosexuality in sex education classes. An educational TV channel recently aired a "Gay for the Deaf" program during which gay deafs were told how to make contact with other deaf homosexuals. A major U.S. city recently announced Gay Pride Day on which municipal offices were closed and a parade for the gays of the city was conducted. In one community, a high school boy was permitted to take his boyfriend to the high school prom. The most popular newspaper advice columns say homosexuality is a moral sexual outlet. In fact, one of the most popular advice columnists recently wrote, "One thing is certain, God made gays just as certainly as God made straights."

One major U.S. city with a population of 660,000 has 100,000 avowed homosexuals. That's one for every 6.6 people. Eliminating the older and younger population, that figure would probably be one homosexual for every three or four people. One conservative estimate suggests that one out of every ten people in the United States is a practicing homosexual. Translated, that means that in an audience of one thousand people, one hundred would be homosexuals.

As homosexuality becomes more visibly a part of our culture, what should be the reaction of the Christian? What should parents teach their children? Is homosexuality a sin, a sickness, or a natural expression for some? For the Christian, the answer does not lie with the sociologists, educators, psychologists, physicians, politicians, judges, or newspaper columinists. The answer lies in the Bible.

Homosexuality and Creation

A second person of the same sex is insufficient to complement the sexual make-up of the first person. God taught us that when He said, "It is not good for the man to be alone; I will make a helper suitable for him" (Genesis 2:18). The Hebrew word for *suitable* literally can mean "according to what is in front of," which might be taken as a reference to the sexual organ of the male. Though it is certainly not limited to physical correspondence, male and female do physically correspond to each other. The female design does not sexually correspond with another female design, nor does the male design with another male design.

Paul was reinforcing the teaching of this creative plan of God when he wrote, "The wife does not have authority over her own body, but the husband does; and likewise also the husband does not have authority over his own body, but the wife does" (1 Corinthians 7:4). The word for *authority* means power. The woman or man does not have power to be sexually satisfied without the corresponding sex. There was no place in God's creative plan for homosexuality. When man needed a corresponding mate, God created an Eve, not a Steve. That's why Paul called male to female sexual relationships "natural" and homosexuality "unnatural" (Romans 1:26, 27). Paul tied the concept of what was natural and unnatural to creation (Romans 1:20).

Homosexuality and the Old Testament

The Old Testament calls homosexuality an abomination:

"You shall not lie with a male as one lies with a female; it is an abomination" (Leviticus 18:22). The Hebrew word for abomination *(toebah)* refers to anything that is against the true nature of a person. God considered homosexuality to be one of those activities that defiled the land (Leviticus 18:27). Some have suggested that this prohibition against homosexuality was a temporary one because it was connected with the paganism of Israel's neighbors. So the only reason God was against it was so the Israelites would not have sexual activities with their homosexual neighbors and be lured to worship their pagan gods.

There are several problems with this explanation: (1) God prohibited homosexual activities with *anyone,* not only with pagans. The next verse in Leviticus (18:23) prohibited intercourse with animals. God certainly did not mean just those animals that belong to the pagan neighbors. (2) The prohibition against homosexuality was carried over into the New Testament, making it clear that this was not a command for one time and one culture only. (3) The command against homosexuality continued throughout the Old Testament (Leviticus 20:13; 1 Kings 14:24; 15:12). (4) Paul took his teaching against homosexuality back to the beginning—to creation—not to the temporary environment of the Israelites in the initial days of conquering the promised land. (5) God destroyed people who committed homosexuality without mentioning their religious practices.

Sodom and Gomorrah were destroyed because of the homosexual activities that permeated those cities. However, that interpretation of the reason God destroyed these cities has recently been challenged. A few years ago, a pro-homosexual leader was the first person to suggest that Sodom and Gomorrah were destroyed because of the absence of hospitality, not because of the presence of homosexuality.

The context denies that hospitality was the issue. Two messengers from God visited Lot, and while they were there, the men of the city arrived with a request, "Where are the men who came to you tonight? Bring them out to us that we may have relations with them" (Genesis 19:5). It has been correctly pointed out that the Hebrew literally says, "Bring them out to us that we may *know* them." The

33

Hebrew word used here is the same word used in the following passages:

And Adam *knew* Eve his wife; and she conceived, and bare Cain . . . (Genesis 4:1, KJV).

And Cain *knew* his wife; and she conceived, and bare Enoch . . . (Genesis 4:17, KJV).

And Adam knew his wife again; and she bare a son, and called his name Seth . . . (Genesis 4:25, KJV).

Behold now, I have two daughters who have not *known* man . . . (Genesis 19:8, KJV).

And the damsel was very fair to look upon, a virgin, neither had any man *known* her . . . (Genesis 24:16, KJV).

And he *knew* her again no more (Genesis 38:26, KJV).

When those men arrived, Lot knew exactly what they wanted to do. That's why he shut the door behind him and said, "Please, my brothers, do not act wickedly" (Genesis 19:6, 7). The Hebrew word for wickedly *(raa)* is used elsewhere to refer to homosexual activities (Judges 19:22, 23). Peter called the men "unprincipled men" with "sensual conduct" and "lawless deeds" (2 Peter 2:6-8). Jude said they "indulged in gross immorality and went after strange flesh" (Jude 7).

Many pro-homosexuality people like to turn to Ezekiel 16:49, 50 to prove that hospitality was the issue.

Behold, this was the guilt of your sister Sodom; she and her daughters had arrogance, abundant food, and careless ease, but she did not help the poor and needy. Thus, they were haughty and committed abominations before Me. Therefore, I removed them when I saw it.

Some suggest that the abomination was lack of care for needy people—no hospitality. But the context does not support that understanding. The lack of care for the needy and the abominations are not the same, but they are related. Both are the results of the desire to satisfy self only. Later in Ezekiel, we read that Sodom had "borne the penalty of your lewdness and abominations" (Ezekiel 16:58). The Hebrew word for lewdness (zimmah) is used elsewhere to describe sexual sins.

But the men of Gibeah rose up against me and surrounded the house at night because of me. They intended to kill me; instead, they ravished my concubine so that she died. And I took hold of my concubine and cut her in pieces and sent her throughout the land of Israel's inheritance; for they have committed a lewd and disgraceful act in Israel (Judges 20:5, 6).

As for your adulteries and your lustful neighings, the lewdness of your prostitution on the hills in the field, I have seen your abominations. Woe to you, O Jerusalem! How long will you remain unclean? (Jeremiah 13:27).

And one has committed abomination with his neighbor's wife, and another has lewdly defiled his daughter-in-law . . . (Ezekiel 22:11).

In the above passages, lewdness is related to rape, adultery, prostitution, and incest. In other passages also, lewdness refers to sexual sins (Ezekiel 23:19-21, 27, 29, 35, 43-49). The abominations of Sodom in Ezekiel 16:50 are the acts of lewdness in Ezekiel 16:58. Lewdness clearly refers to sexual activities.

Sodom is used often as an example for other cities and countries (Deuteronomy 29:23; 32:32; Isaiah 1:9, 10; 3:9; 13:19; Jeremiah 23:14; 50:40; Lamentations 4:6; Ezekiel 16:46-56; Amos 4:11; Zephaniah 2:9; Matthew 10:15; 11:23, 24; Romans 9:29; 2 Peter 2:6; Jude 7; Revelation 11:8). We must not take Sodom's sin lightly. If we become like them, we will be destroyed as they were, for their sin was a sin of rebellion against the Lord and His Presence. In fact, it violates the image of God that is present in another person. If we continue to do that, we will stumble as Jerusalem and Judah did.

For Jerusalem has stumbled and Judah has fallen, because their speech and their actions are against the Lord, to rebel against His glorious presence. The expression of their faces bears witness against them. And they display their sin like Sodom; they do not even conceal it. Woe to them! For they have brought evil on themselves (Isaiah 3:8, 9).

In another Old Testament passage, some men of a city

35

attempted homosexual relations with a man; however, the host offered his virgin daughter to them instead (Judges 19:22-30). It is difficult for us to understand that offer. The host certainly felt an obligation to his guest. But could it also be possible that the host considered the improper sexual relations with the opposite sex to be a lesser evil than homosexual relations?

The Old Testament certainly does not give any positive support to homosexuality. It even condemns transvestism—dressing in the clothes of the opposite sex (Deuteronomy 22:5).

The New Testament and Homosexuality

Homosexuality in the New Testament is considered to be one of those unrighteous acts that prevents people from inheriting the kingdom of God.

> Or do you know that the unrighteous shall not inherit the kingdom of God? Do not be deceived; neither fornicators, nor idolaters, nor adulterers, nor effeminate, nor homosexuals, nor thieves, nor the covetous, nor drunkards, nor revilers, nor swindlers, shall inherit the kingdom of God (1 Corinthians 6:9, 10).

The Greek word for fornicators is *porne* (from which we get "porno"). It is a Greek word that refers to *any* sexual sin. Following the use of this word is a brief list of sexual sins—adultery, effeminacy, and homosexuality. A person who is not cleansed of any one of those sexual sins will be excluded from Heaven. "Outside are the dogs and the sorcerers and the immoral persons *(porne)* and the murderers and the idolaters, and everyone who loves and practices lying" (Revelation 22:15). The "immoral persons" includes the homosexuals and effeminate.

The Greek word for homosexuals *(arsenokoites)* comes from the word for male *(arsen)* and bed *(koite*—from which we get our word *coitus*—sexual intercourse). The word effeminate *(malakos)* refers to those men and boys who allow themselves to be misused sexually. While one is active (homosexual), the other is passive (effeminate).

Homosexuality is not restricted to the male population. Lesbianism is also condemned, "For this reason God gave them over to degrading passions; for their women exchanged the natural functions for that which is unnatural" (Romans 1:26).

Every description about people in Romans 1:18-32 is related to the homosexual activities in Romans 1:25-27. It is ungodliness and unrighteousness performed by people who suppress the truth in unrighteousness (Romans 1:18). What truth do they suppress? God's creation (Romans 1:19-20). Such people do not honor God with their sexuality. They do not give thanks. In fact, they rebel against their sexuality rather than give thanks for it. They have different ideas about their sexuality, but become futile in their speculations (Romans 1:21). They dishonor their bodies (Romans 1:24). Their passions are degrading and unnatural (Romans 1:27). Their minds are depraved (Romans 1:28). They not only practice wrong, but give hearty approval to others who practice wrong (Romans 1:32).

Homosexuality is one of the many sins for which the Law was made. It stands contrary to sound teaching.

But we know that the Law is good, if one uses it lawfully, realizing the fact that the law is not made for a righteous man, but for those who are lawless and rebellious, for the ungodly and sinners, for the unholy and profane, for those who kill their fathers or mothers, for murderers and immoral men and homosexuals and kidnappers and liars and perjurers, and whatever else is contrary to sound teaching (1 Timothy 1:8-10).

"Sound teaching" is an interesting phrase. The word for sound *(ugies)* refers to something that is *whole, healthy, well, cured.* Sound teaching is that teaching which brings wellness, healthiness, wholeness, and cure to people. Homosexuality prevents a person from being well, whole, or cured. That's the reason God teaches against homosexuality. He loves us and wants only what is good for us.

Homosexuality and Jesus

Some have suggested that Jesus was not opposed to homosexuality since He did not directly condemn it; however, that is an argument from silence. That same line of reasoning would conclude that Jesus was not opposed to incest, public nakedness, sorcery, strife, jealousy, and several other vices, since He did not directly condemn them.

The Alternative Life-Style

While many suggest that homosexuality/lesbianism is an accepted alternative life-style, the Bible does not agree. The only accepted alternative life-style to male/female sexual relations within marriage is celibacy. Jesus spotlighted that alternative when He said:

> Not everyone can accept this teaching, but only those to whom it has been given. For some are eunuchs because they were born that way; others were made that way by men; and others have renounced marriage because of the kingdom of heaven. The one who can accept this should accept it (Matthew 19:11, 12, NIV).

Paul also emphasized the celibacy alternative when he wrote to the Corinthians about alternatives to marriage:

> Yet I wish that all men were even as I myself am. However, each man has his own gift from God, one in this manner, and another in that. But I say to the unmarried and to widows that it is good for them if they remain even as I. But if they do not have self-control, let them marry; for it is better to marry than to burn (1 Corinthians 7:7-9).

And that's just after Paul spoke against homosexuality (1 Corinthians 6:9, 10).

Homosexuality—Which Kind

Some people talk about two different kinds of homosexuals—the *invert* homosexual and the *overt* homosexual. The *inverted* homosexual is that person who does not have sexual desire for the opposite sex, but does not practice sexual acts with his own sex. However, the *overted* homosexual does practice sexual acts with his own sex. The inverted has only a homosexual orientation, while the overted engages in homosexual activity.

While that distinction is common among the pro-homosexual camp, it is not a distinction made in the Bible. The person without sexual attraction for the opposite sex is *not* a homosexual. He is simply a person with a God-given charisma for celibacy. He should not look upon himself as a potential homosexual, nor should others so look upon him. Unless such a person understands that he has charisma from God (1 Corinthians 7:7), he may become a prey to

38

homosexuals and begin thinking that homosexuality is natural for him. In fact, pro-homosexuals teach that the person who is not sexually attracted to the opposite sex is not giving up his natural function by turning to his own sex. In fact, heterosexuality would be the unnatural act for him. Thus, according to pro-homosexuals, Romans 1:24-27 does not apply to the inverted homosexual. It applies only to those people who have a natural attraction to the opposite sex, but exchange it for activities with the same sex. Even many pro-homosexuals would say that is perversion, but not inversion. But the Bible lists no acceptable and unacceptable categories of homosexuality.

Pro-homosexuals teach that it is not wrong for a person who "naturally" feels attracted to his own sex to be a functioning homosexual. However, feeling something is right doesn't make it right. Solomon wrote, "There is a way which seems right to a man, but its end is the way of death" (Proverbs 14:12). (See also Proverbs 12:15; 16:2, 25; 21:2.)

Being tempted to act out desires is not restricted to homosexuality. *Every* person is tempted by his *desires.* That's what temptation is all about. (James 1:14—note the word *lust* is really the neutral word *desires.* We are always tempted by the desires we have.)

Just because we have certain desires doesn't mean it is natural and right to express them. We are to control our desires, not let them control us.

> Let us behave decently, as in the daytime, not in orgies and drunkenness, not in sexual immorality and debauchery, not in dissension and jealousy. Rather, clothe yourselves with the Lord Jesus Christ, and do not think about how to gratify the desires of the sinful nature (Romans 13:13, 14, NIV).

Is it wrong to have homosexual desires? No! Is it wrong to be tempted to engage in homosexual acts! No! It is what we do with those desires that makes the difference. "But the things that proceed out of the mouth come from the heart, and those defile the man" (Matthew 15:18). However, it is also wrong to nurture our desires mentally so we "dream" them. That is, we mentally engage in wrong deeds even though we do not physically engage in them. "The devising of folly is sin . . ." (Proverbs 24:9). That's why Jesus spoke against mentally scheming as well as physically doing wrong (Matthew 5:28).

The more we dwell on our evil desires, the more easily the internal and external environment can provide us the rationalization we think we need to carry out those wrong desires. Then we get carried away. "But each one is tempted when he is carried away and enticed by his own lust (desire). Then when lust (desire) has conceived, it gives birth to sin; and when sin is accomplished, it brings forth death" (James 1:14, 15).

Consequently, we must manage our minds with positive mind-control:

> Since, then, you have been raised with Christ, set your hearts on things above, where Christ is seated at the right hand of God. Set your minds on things above, not on earthly things. For you died, and your life is now hidden with Christ in God (Colossians 3:1-3, NIV).

> Put to death, therefore, whatever belongs to your earthly nature: sexual immorality, impurity, lust, evil desires and greed, which is idolatry (Colossians 3:5, NIV).

> Finally, brothers, whatever is true, whatever is noble, whatever is right, whatever is pure, whatever is lovely, whatever is admirable—if anything is excellent or praiseworthy—think about such things. Whatever you have learned or received or heard from me, or seen in me—put it into practice. And the God of peace will be with you (Philippians 4:8, 9, NIV).

Homosexual Causes and Cures

What causes homosexuality? Some say it is genetically caused. But scientific research does not support that. Homosexuals are not biologically different from heterosexuals. In fact, clinical studies reveal that some homosexuals have more male hormones than the average heterosexual. Changing the amount of hormones given to people in tests did not change their sex desires and preferences. It appears that homosexuals are imitating a sex they do not possess.

Homosexuality is sin caused by temptation. Various kinds of environments can augment the lure of the temptation and reduce resistance to it. For instance, there is the external environment. Studies show that a boy who has a close-binding relationship with his mother while at the same time has an indifferent father may be more likely to identify with the parent of the opposite sex in dress and mannerisms. People who live in a highly concentrated homosexual population may be more likely to engage in some homosexual acts.

There is also the internal environment. Studies show that an extra female chromosome in a male or an extra male chromosome in a female or the absence of the normal complement of sex chromosomes can affect the development of sexual organs and can affect sexual behavior; however, the chromosome differences do not automatically cause homosexuality. But people with one of the above internal environments can be taught that he is a homosexual by nature and then live out his "education."

Although the command against homosexuality did not change throughout the Bible, the way to handle it did. The Old Testament called for the death penalty (Leviticus 20:13) or expulsion from the land (1 Kings 15:12; 22:46). But the New Testament calls for a change in the person.

But can change happen? Of course! The idea of once a homosexual, always a homosexual, is not valid. Remaining a homosexual is a result of desire. Practicing homosexuals have changed their sex orientation through therapy that does such things as devalue homosexual impulses, value the opposite sex, and enhance a person's estimate of his own sexual identity as a male or female. Paul talked about a church that had former homosexuals in it. But they were washed, sanctified, and justified in the name of the Lord Jesus Christ and in the Spirit of Christ (1 Corinthians 6:9-11). God specializes in making us new creations in Christ (2 Corinthians 5:17). What is not possible in our culture is always possible in Christ. However, the homosexual must believe that Christ can do it, want to be transformed, confess of wrong to God, repent of wrong, and confess Jesus as the Master of beliefs and behavior.

Misconceptions about Homosexuals

Many misconceptions about homosexuals are popular. Here are some:
1. You can always tell one by his mannerisms.
2. A homosexual tends to molest children.

3. Homosexuals have a low self-esteem.

4. Homosexuals are unreliable on the job.

All of the above depend more upon the individual than upon his sex choice. However, homosexuals do tend to pervert teenagers to their life-style, do not have long-term relationships, and encourage the spread of venereal disease.

The Church and Homosexuality

The church should not condone what God condemns. She must share a revelational, redemptive ministry by teaching the truth that homosexuality is sin, but receiving repentant homosexuals who put on Jesus Christ as brothers and sisters in Christ.

The church must not treat the person with the attitude of "once in sin, always in sin." To shun a former homosexual is to fail to forgive whom God has forgiven. When God reconciles a person to himself, He demands that we do the same. To fail to do so is a sin in the same category as homosexuality. One is no less a sin than the other.

May the church believe and express the truth that God's grace is greater than man's disgrace. May every church be able to say what Paul said: "And such were some of you; but you were washed, but you were sanctified, but you were justified in the name of the Lord Jesus Christ, and in the Spirit of our God" (1 Corinthians 6:11).

For Your Consideration or Discussion

1. Suppose a good friend confided in you that he/she is homosexual. What would be your immediate reaction? Would it change the way you feel about that person? Would it change the nature of your friendship? If so, why?

2. Do you draw a distinction between practicing homosexuals and persons with homosexual desires who do not act out these desires? Would you respond differently to the former than to the latter? If so, why?

3. A homosexual is a person with a problem. Do you consider that problem to be a sickness or a sin? Or both? Share your reasons for your position.

4. A homosexual is a person with a problem. A human being is a person with a problem or problems. Therefore, is a homosexual any different than any other human being? Discuss your feelings about this question.
5. Is the problem of the homosexual primarily *his/her* problem or a problem generated by the attitude of society toward homosexuals? Or both? Discuss it.
6. Note: "Exodus" is an international Christian ministry to homosexuals. For information on the Exodus ministry nearest you, write Dr. Bruce Parmenter at 1509 W. John, Champaign, IL 61820, or call him at (217) 352-3033.

Chapter 4

CONTRACEPTION

"Is it right or wrong to use contraceptives?" Many married couples are asking this question. But beyond that personal issue are emerging many other issues: (1) What type of contraceptive is "right" or "wrong"? (2) Should the local, state, or Federal government distribute contraceptives? If so, to whom? (3) Should the government enforce contraception for certain persons such as the retarded, habitual criminals, or others?

Contraception literally means *against or contrary (contra) to a beginning process (ception).* It is erroneous to put the use of contraceptives into the same category as abortion. Abortion terminates life which has already begun. Contraception prevents the beginning of life. While one is termination, the other is prevention.

The use of contraceptives is not modern. Contraceptives were used in the Greek and Roman Empires. However, neither is the opposition to contraception modern. The church in early times opposed the use of contraceptives. Some church scholars in the second through the fourth centuries taught that a wife and a husband should have intercourse only for the purpose of having children. Some taught it was wrong for a husband to have intercourse with his pregnant wife since the sex organs are only for procreation, and intercourse during pregnancy can not beget a child. One modern scholar who has researched the history of the churches' attitude toward contraception found only one statement prior to the sixteenth century that allowed intercourse between a husband and wife for the purpose of pleasure.

The Roman Catholic Church has been a consistent leader

in speaking out against the use of contraceptives. That church believes that the only legitimate use of birth control is the rhythm method. An ancient Roman Catholic Canon called for the same number of penances for contraception as for homicide. Augustine spoke against the sin of intercourse for pleasure. Roman Catholic scholars taught that the use of contraceptives was a sin against nature, and Thomas Aquinas said that "sin against nature" was the worst sexual sin of all. Bernardine even said that it would be better for a woman to have sexual relations with her father than for her to have "unnatural" relations with her husband. Pope Sixtus V declared that anyone who gave contraceptives to a woman should be excommunicated.

With the rise of the birth control movement toward the end of the nineteenth century, the contraception issue began to come out of the closet. However, acceptance of contraceptives came slowly. For instance, Massachusetts outlawed a physician from prescribing contraceptives. Connecticut had a law that forbade a husband and wife from using contraceptives when having intercourse. A Federal law banned the mailing of information about contraception on the grounds that such information is obscene and filthy. During the 1960s, each of the above laws was changed. Since that time, contraceptives have been easily accessible. Many communities make them available to unmarried teenagers—and even to preteens.

The moral question continues. Is the use of contraceptives, beyond the rhythm method, Biblically right or wrong?

Contraception and the Bible

The church's opposition against the use of birth control has come from at least three understandings:
1. The Bible teaches against the use of birth control as in the incident of Onan, who spilled his seed on the ground and thus displeased God.
2. Man is born with original sin, thus his desires for sex beyond having children are depraved. That makes the sex act beyond the procreation purpose depraved.
3. The only reason for sexual intercourse is for the producing of children.

These three positions need to be considered. It is true

that Onan displeased the Lord in his actions (Genesis 38:10). But there was far more to that displeasure than just the fact that Onan spilled his semen on the ground.

In order to help preserve family names and estates, God established the levirate marriage. This was the marriage of a man to his brother's widow.

> When brothers live together and one of them dies and has no son, the wife of the deceased shall not be married outside the family to a strange man. Her husband's brother shall go in to her and take her to himself as wife and perform the duty of a husband's brother to her. And it shall be that the first-born whom she bears shall assume the name of his dead brother, that his name may not be blotted out from Israel (Deuteronomy 25:5, 6).

It was considered shameful for a man to fail to carry out this responsibility for his deceased brother.

> But if the man does not desire to take his brother's wife, then his brother's wife shall go up to the gate to the elders and say, "My husband's brother refuses to establish a name for his brother in Israel; he is not willing to perform the duty of a husband's brother to me." Then the elders of this city shall summon him and speak to him. And if he persists and says, "I do not desire to take her," then his brother's wife shall come to him in the sight of the elders, and pull his sandal off his foot and spit in his face; and she shall declare, "Thus it is done to the man who does not build up his brother's house." And in Israel his name shall be called, "The house of him whose sandal is removed" (Deuteronomy 25:7-10).

Onan's brother had died without having children (Genesis 38:6, 7). The father of the two sons ordered Onan to carry out his responsibilities. "Go in to your brother's wife, and perform your duty as a brother-in-law to her, and raise up offspring for your brother" (Genesis 38:8). Onan could have refused and then have borne the shame, but instead he played the role of a hypocrite. He pretended to be carrying out a duty, but he didn't. The text is clear that Onan did not want to raise a child *for his brother.* "And Onan knew that the offspring would not be his; so it came about that when he went in to his brother's wife, he wasted his seed on the ground, in order not to give offspring to his brother" (Genesis 38:9).

Onan's sin was in disobeying both God's command and

his father's order, selfishness, and playing the role of a hypocrite. That incident has nothing to do with whether or not a married couple can use contraceptives today or even then. In fact, the Bible is silent concerning the use of contraceptives.

The doctrine that man is born in a depraved state is not universally accepted. If that doctrine were true, even the depraved man's desire to have children would be evil. In his total depravity, he would want children for unwholesome reasons. There is no hint in the Bible that relates the idea of original sin or total depravity to a married couple's sexual activities.

The position that the only purpose for sexual intercourse is procreation is a "telescoping" position. By that I mean that some have zoomed their interpretative telescopes onto a few verses and missed the other verses. It is true that God said, "Be fruitful and multiply" (Genesis 1:28), but He did not say that is the *only* reason for intercourse. In fact, the first reason God stated for creating another sex that would correspond to what is in front of the male was to answer the man's loneliness (Genesis 2:18). The first stated result of intercourse was that "they shall become one flesh" not "they shall become parents." If having children is the only reason for intercourse, isn't it strange that the violation of that was never mentioned as a reason why God was against adultery, homosexuality, or intercourse with animals.

The Bible reveals many reasons for intercourse, not just one. Here are some of them:

1. *Unity.* This is one of the ideas of "one flesh" (Genesis (2:24). The two become united—emotionally. Intercourse is not to be an added tack-on just because we want some children, but a crowning moment that captures the love, appreciation, and mutuality of all the other moments of the day. Intercourse is far more than just the physical act of a coitus. Thus, a meaningful sex life between a husband and wife does not depend only upon how the two get into bed at night, but also how they get out of it in the morning and their interpersonal relationships with each other. That's why it is difficult for one mate to be ignored or mistreated outside the bedroom and then feel that he/she is not being used in the love act.

2. *Communication.* One of the Hebew words for the love act is "know," because the intimate love act is communication that seeks to know and be known beyond surface levels. It is love shared, not just love spoken. The love act is a relational attitude, not just a procreational activity.

3. *The relieving of tension.* What happens when a tea kettle or pressure cooker is on the burner, but there is no outlet for the steam to escape? The vessel will eventually blow up. People are like that. We are always on a burner. Sometimes it may be turned up high and sometimes it may be a low burn. But either way, pressure builds in people's lives. God has given to us many "Godufactured" outlets to relieve pressure. Work, exercise, talk, prayer, worship, and sleep are some of our natural outlets. But in addition to those is the sexual love act between a husband and a wife. Outside of marriage, intercourse builds tension; but inside marriage, it relieves tension if the relational dimension is allowed to be a part of the intimacy.

We see a Biblical reference to this function of marital sex in Isaac's life. Isaac's mother had died. That created anxiety. Then we read about the activity that comforted him. "Then Isaac brought her into his mother Sarah's tent, and took Rebekah, and she became his wife; and he loved her; thus Isaac was comforted after his mother's death" (Genesis 24:67). The word "loved" is one of the Hebrew ways to describe marital sex. The word that described this incident in the Greek translation of the Old Testament is *agape.* Agape love is always unselfish love. It sees a need in another person and moves to meet it. That's the way sexual love between a husband and wife should be. When it seeks to meet the other person's need, it is truly relational and fulfilling.

A fine description of agape love is found in 1 Corinthians 13:4-8. That kind of love is to dominate every aspect of married life—including the sexual aspect. Each husband and wife should measure their sex-love by the aspects of this description:

> Love is patient, love is kind, and is not jealous; love does not brag and it is not arrogant, does not act unbecomingly; it does not seek its own, is not provoked, does not take into account a wrong suffered, does not rejoice in unrighteousness, but re-

joices with the truth; bears all things, believes all things, hopes all things, endures all things. Love never fails; but if there are gifts of prophecy, they will be done away; if there are tongues, they will cease; if there is knowledge, it will be done away.

Do we allow all of those aspects to be a part of our sexual love with our mates? Are we really patient, kind, and not seeking our own way? When we allow our sexual activities to be an expression of agape love, that activity relieves tension.

So the next time you notice that your mate has had a tough day—the burner has been turned up high—that's the time to put on that special negligee (or if you are a man whatever). There is no greater muscle relaxing and mind settling activity that a husband and wife can give to each other.

4. *Pleasure.* If most couples were asked, "Is sex a duty, a dread, or a delight?" I wonder how they would respond—particularly the wife. I'm afraid many would say, "It's a dread. You know, 'For better or for worse,' and this is one of those 'worse.' " And certainly many wives would think that way if they believe the only reason for the sex act is to have children.

But it doesn't have to be a dread. God wants it to be a delight. He created sex partly for pleasure, but not selfish pleasure—for mutual recreation, not just for procreation. We see this dimension being expressed by Sarah. When Sarah was eighty-nine years old, she received the news that she was going to have a baby—her *first.* Just think about the human dimensions to that. Eighty-nine years old and she's going to have morning sickness for the first time in her life. Eighty-nine years old and she starts getting a supply of *Pampers.* Abraham was one hundred years old when the baby was born. Can't you see him checking the time between labor pains with his magnifying glass, and can't you see him taking his ninety-year old wife to the hospital and asking whether or not Medicaid would pay for the nursery?

How would Sarah handle news like that at age eighty nine? How would you handle it at forty-nine? (I can tell you how I handled it a when I was forty-two.) Here's how Sarah handled it. She "laughed to herself" (Genesis 18:12). Laughed? That's right! Why? Because she was old? That's hardly the reason to laugh. But there's more to it. "After I become old, shall I have pleasure, my lord being old also?" The word pleasure is one of the Hebrew descriptions for the sex act between a husband and wife. Sarah's laugh must have been a delightful glee of anticipating of the love sharing act with her husband. And she saw that as pleasure. What a fantastic response! But she could never have responded with *that* word had not both her husband and she allowed that dimension of their life together to be pleasurable. That calls for mutual caring and sharing in meeting the other person's needs—*agape* love.

5. *A natural environment for expressing mutual admiration.* The non-verbal ways of saying, "I love you," need to be backed up with verbal expressions of love. The bedroom intimacies between a husband and wife provide the natural environment for the verbal expressions of appreciation.

Nowhere do we see this better than in the Song of Solomon. That entire Bible book records the admiration that a husband and wife have for each other. Every married person ought to read it with the questions, "How long has it been since I've talked with my mate like that?" Here are just a few of the gems from that book:

Wife: "May he kiss me with the kisses of his mouth. For your love is better than wine" (1:2). *In the culture of that day, wine was a prized substance, considered almost "essential" as well as refreshing. The wife here indicates that nothing is more satisfying to her than being sexually intimate with her husband.*

Wife: "Your oils have a pleasing fragrance" (1:3). *Now fellows, she won't say that to us if we don't shower and use deodorant and after shave lotion.*

Husband: "To me my darling, you are like my mare among the chariots of Pharaoh" (1:9). *Now fellows, we need to make some changes due to different cultures. I wouldn't dare say to Julia, "Darling, you remind of an old horse." While animals were precious then, today it may be cars. Do our wives see us appreciating them more than the Pintos, Colts, Mustangs, or Jaguars?*

Husband: "How beautiful you are, my darling, how beautiful you are! Your eyes are like doves" (1:15).

Wife: "How handsome you are, my beloved, and so pleasant! Indeed our couch is luxuriant!" (1:16). *Isn't their mutual admiration beautiful to read?*

Wife: "Like an apple tree among the trees of the forest, so is my beloved among the young men. In his shade I took great delight and sat down, and his fruit was sweet to my taste" (2:3). *Here's a wife totally satisfied with her husband. She compares the bedroom to a banquet hall. It's enjoyable.* "He has brought me to his banquet hall, and his banner over me is love" (2:4).

Husband: "Your hair is like a flock of goats that have descended from Mount Gilead" (4:1). *We'd better change something there, fellows. I wouldn't dare say, "Darling your hair looks like a bunch of goats." Perhaps, "Your hair is like mink and silk merged together." For several verses the husband praises his wife's body. Do we?*

Husband: "You have made my heart beat faster, my sister, my bride; you have made my heart beat faster with a single glance of your eyes, with a single strand of your necklace" (4:9). *Here's a guy about to have a cardiac arrest over his own wife. Fantastic!*

Wife: "I am my beloved's, and his desire is for me" (7:10).

All of the song of Solomon reads like that. But why is that in the Holy Bible? Because that's the kind of model relationship God would like to see happen between every husband and wife.

6. *To complete the creative design of the other person.* Paul communicated that when he wrote: "The wife does not have authority over her own body, but the husband does; and likewise also the husband does not have authority over his own body, but the wife does" (1 Corinthians 7:4).

7. *To help protect your mate (and yourself) from the temptations of Satan.* So Paul in 1 Corinthians 7:5 wrote: (a) "Stop depriving one another" (That is a command just as sacred as Acts 2:38.) (b) "except by agreement." The Greek word *agreement* is *symphone* from which we get our word *symphony. Symphony* literally means *sounds (phonic) that blend together (sym).*

The symphonic kind of agreement is always *mutual* agreement. No person has the Biblical right to withhold sexual intimacies from his/her mate. It is Biblically wrong to keep claiming, "I've got a headache," or, "I'm too tired." The mutual agreement for abstinence for a time is "that you may devote yourselves to prayer." I have not yet heard a couple name prayer as their reason for abstinence.

Paul does not permit prolonged abstinence, "and come together again lest Satan tempt you because of your lack of self-control." Satan knows how we are created and will try to take advantage of those situations in which husband and wife are not mutually sharing their physical expressions of love with each other. And Satan has a lot of lovely people in the world he can use to help take advantage of those situations. Consequently, sharing physical love with our mates helps to protect them and us from the onslaughts of the devil and his schemes.

When we consider all the purposes for sexual intimacy between a husband and wife, it is no wonder Paul wrote, "Let the husband fulfill his duty to his wife, and likewise also the wife to her husband" (1 Corinthians 7:3). The word *duty* is a misleading translation. The Greek word *(opheile)* means a *debt*—an I.O.U. A husband and wife actually owe to each other the expressions of physical intimacies. Because of all the ways it serves the other person, it is a debt that we should never consider "paid in full."

While the use of contraceptives does prevent the procreation dimension of sexual intimacy, it may enhance the other dimensions. While we are to replenish the earth, there is no hint in the Bible that that should be the purpose every time or even most of the times that husbands and wives share sexual love with each other. If procreation were God's only reason, why would He design the woman in a way that she could get pregnant only three days out of thirty?

The fact that God gave us the ability to beget and conceive children does not mean He takes away from us responsibility in handling that ability. We are to be stewards with God's grace, not stupid with it. To produce babies as quickly as our biological functions will permit without regard to our abilities to care for them is irresponsible. To withhold sex until a couple wants to have another baby violates the commands of 1 Corinthians 7:3-5. To refuse to have any children for selfish reasons is also to act irresponsibly.

The decision to use or not use contraceptives is a decision each couple has the Biblical freedom to decide for themselves—as well as which kind of contraceptive to use. The decision should be based upon faith. A person who believes that the use of contraceptives is sin should not use them until he has settled that issue in his mind. If we do something thinking it is sin, then we have sinned in our attitudes (see chapter 11, on neutral issues).

There is nothing Biblically wrong with planned parenthood—provided a life that has begun has not been aborted. God has given couples the freedom to plan for children. However, no plan is 100% effective. Couples who get a "surprise" announcement from a doctor should become responsible in planning for the arrival of a baby made in the image of God. An "accident" does not give us divine authorization for an abortion.

But how about contraceptives for single people? In a recent letter to a syndicated columnist, a teenager wrote a letter telling about her neglect to use contraceptives, which she followed up with the decision to abort. The advice columnist commented in her letter and reinforced that teenagers should use contraceptives. Neither the teenager nor the columnist mentioned that sexual intercourse should be restricted to married partners and that abstinence by teen-agers prevents pregnancy.

It is Biblically wrong for unmarried persons to engage in intercourse. That is the issue—not the use or non-use of contraceptives by singles. We are walking down the wrong road when we distribute contraceptives to the unmarried. That road heightens permissiveness. And we are walking down the wrong path to legally enforce the use of con-traceptives by certain persons such as the retarded or habitually criminal. That road heightens the philosophy of engineering a "super" race. It is the kind of philosophy that led Hitler to want to force sterilization on all Jews. Where do we draw the line on forced use of contraceptives once we've started in that direction?

Whether we do or do not use contraceptives, the Chris-tian should adopt and maintain the philosophy that sex is a blessing from God. Sexual intercourse between a husband and wife is not dirty. It was designed from the purest and cleanest mind that has or will ever exist—God's. It is a "many splendored thing" as it meets many needs of a couple.

At the same time, a couple should adopt the philosophy that children are a blessing from God. Our ancient forefathers talked about their children as children God gave to them (Genesis 33:5; 48:4). Great people of old under-stood that children are a blessing. And indeed they are. Listen to the psalmist:

> Behold, children are a gift of the Lord; the fruit of the womb is a reward. Like arrows in the hand of a warrior, so are the children of one's youth. How blessed is the man whose quiver is full of them (Psalm 127:3-5).

For Your Consideration or Discussion

1. Imagine yourself talking to an engaged couple who have sought your advice on marriage. They express their opin-ion that God did not intend for married couples to use contraceptives. How would you reply?
2. Imagine yourself talking to a good friend who is a member of the Roman Catholic faith. That person says that the

rhythm method is not a contraceptive method. Would you agree? If not, how would you support your position?

3. Assume that Christian parents have an unmarried teen-aged child who is sexually active and who has told his/her parents that he/she does not intend to stop. Assume that the parents, indeed, cannot get the child to stop and that they decide then to advise the child to use a contraceptive. Would you agree with such advice or not? Discuss it.

4. Assume that a young Christian married couple tells you that they have decided to have no children because they prefer to remain childless as a life-style. Would you agree? Why or why not?

Chapter 5

THE DATING GAME
AND TEENAGE SEX

Dating—what an interesting Western practice. It can be either a delight or a drudgery. I never thought the time would ever come when I would go on my first date. But it did. Then I never thought the time would ever come when that first date got over. But it did. Those three hours seemed like three years.

There are some myths about dating that need to be explored.

1. *Self Worth.* Dating can help self-esteem. If you're a girl, it helps if you're being asked. If you're a guy it helps if your call gets a yes answer. But the dating game can also hurt self-esteem. It hurts terribly if you're never asked, get stood up often, or have the receiver slammed down in your ear.

Remember those "mountain-top" feelings when you were among the first to be chosen for the spelling bee, the neighborhood ball team, and the birthday party? And remember those "crawl-into-the-hole" feelings when you stood alone—the last person to be picked and no one really wanted you—and you knew it? Well, those same kind of feelings emerge again during the dating game.

Do you know why the dating game affects self-esteem? Because we've learned to evaluate self worth at the teen level by the dating test. A few years ago, a teenager on her fifteenth birthday left a suicide note that said, "If I fail in what I do, I fail in what I am. Good-bye." That teenager was living the myth that many people have lived. The myth is this—self worth is measured by our activities. And for many teenagers, dating is one of the priority activities that measures worth.

Our worth is not tied to what we do, but to who we are. Each person is unique. There are no two people alike. No one in the world—in the past or in the future—will have your fingerprints or your voice. We are one of a kind.

When a person is born today, he receives a package of characteristics from his father and mother. His father and mother have the capability of transmitting characteristics of all of their ancestors on both sides. That provides an unbelievable combination of possibilities. When a person is born today, there are 240,000,000,000,000,000,000,000 (plus 250 billion *more* zeros) different possible combinations of which he will become just one. If someone had a full-time job (forty hours a week) just writing down the zeros, it would take him forty-five years. No wonder you are the only person who has ever lived, or will ever live, who is just like you. And that makes you incalculatively worthy.

What is given the most worth on earth? The rarest items. Find something that is the only one in the world, and you've found a gold mine—whether it is a penny or a stamp. And the penny or stamp doesn't have to *do* anything but exist. Now look into the mirror. There's your gold mine! That's why Jesus said that if a man gained the whole world—got all the houses, boats, oil wells, and the rest deeded to him—but lost his own self, he made a bad trade. He traded off the valuable for the cheap. He was ripped off by the greatest and oldest con game in human history. And a lot of people have fallen for that con game, because that game has the master con artist still working it—the devil. He's a master at making people feel worthless. And he loves to use the dating game to con teenagers.

2. *Getting to Know You.* We get to know one another on dates—right? Wrong! You never really get to know a person just by dating. Dating is too artificial. We are putting up our best front on dates. We are a bit different on a date than around the house when the "dreamboat" isn't watching.

That's one reason the majority of people do not date the way Americans do prior to marriage. In many cultures, dating is prohibited prior to marriage. In fact, many people do not spend any time together until the marriage. They don't "fall in love" first and then get married. They marry and are committed to love each other because they are married. And the divorce rate is lower in most of those cultures than in ours.

In some other cultures, the dates must include all members of the family. A friend of mine from Thailand dated that way. On every date, the brothers and sisters and parents tagged along. How utterly boring, I thought. So I asked him, "How did you like that, Sammy?"

And he said, "Great."

I thought, "You've got to be kidding!"

But he wasn't. In fact, he made sense to me. He said, "I've dated many girls in the United States, but I never got to know them. But when the brothers, sisters, mother, and father are along, you get to really know that girl as you observe how she acts and reacts not only to you, but also to her family in many different kinds of experiences."

3. *I'll date, but not marry.* If you do not want to marry him, then don't date him. Many people have married into religions, families, and divorces that they did not want. But dating eventually led to walking down the aisle.

4. *I'll pet, but not "go all the way."* That philosophy has got a lot of people into trouble. Petting is to intercourse what the first drink is to alcoholism. It can develop gradually. And it does. I've counselled pregnant teenagers who said, "But I'm not *that* kind of girl."

I replied, "You are *that* kind of girl. Every girl is *that* kind of girl. That's the way God made girls." That's a shock to many people. But it's true, and our teenage girls and boys need to hear it.

God made boys to be stimulated by sight and touch. One picture on a billboard with a scantily-dressed girl selling garlic can set up tingling sensations in a guy. But girls are different. They are not aroused quickly, but they are not dead. A girl who allows petting to begin may think like this: "I'll let this go so far; then I'll say no." That's a good commitment to have. But it's a tough one to stick with. As the petting continues, the mind is saying no, but changes start to take place inside the body. As the petting continues, the mind still says no, but the body starts to say, "Ummmm, nice." As it continues, the mind still says no, but the body starts to say, "Well, maybe." As the petting progresses, the mind still says no, but the body eventually says yes. At that point, the mind is no longer deciding—the body is. While the petting progressed, the body was internally getting ready for intercourse. That's how God made women. As petting continues, they cannot stop their bodies from saying, "Ummmm, well, maybe, yes." When a girl allows her body to get to the place that it says yes while her mind is saying no, she has put herself under far too much pressure. She doesn't *have* to cave in; but when she does, she cannot say, "I'm not *that* kind of girl."

Since a boy is stimulated by sight and touch, it is unkind for a girl to contribute to his stimulation and even escalate it by allowing petting to progress. That plays with his emotions in a way that she has no right to do.

But how can a teenage girl help control the petting situation. Here are some practical suggestions: (1) Don't date an international Don Jaun. He is the guy with *Roman* (roamin') hands and *Russian* (rushin') fingers. (2) If your date starts petting, make it very clear that you will not tolerate it. Don't be taken in by, "If you love me . . ." lines. If he loved you, he wouldn't push. If he persists, you might say, "Just a minute. Let me first call my folks and explain to them what you want to do, and if they say it's OK, we'll continue." (3) Remember, petting is to intercourse what the first drink is to alcoholism. And every girl is *that* kind of girl.

Practical Dating Suggestions

1. *Vary the person.* A teenager is too young to be restricted to dating one person all the time. We mature as we relate to other people. It is important not to narrow our relationships to too few people. It is important to relate to people who are not identical with our personalities. A person who doesn't talk much needs to be in the presence of people who talk more. A person who is intellectual without much common sense needs to spend some time with a more practical person. A person who doesn't laugh much needs to be with people who do. In this way, we help mature and balance each other. Proverbs says, "Iron sharpens iron, so one man sharpens another" (Proverbs 27:17).

2. *Vary the experience.* By that, I mean don't go on the same kind of dates all the time. You can never know a person unless you see him in many different kinds of experiences. So the more varied the experiences, the more you can know about a person. If you have been accustomed to

private dates (just the two of you), go on some double or triple dates. It's important to observe how each of you relates to *other* people when you are together. Are you all of a sudden a "nobody" when other people are around? Does he crawl inside a shell when other people are around? Sometimes go on "social" dates. That is a date with many people involved—not just two or four. Vary what you do on a date. If you have been spectators, such as viewing movies or sports, become participants, such as bowling, playing miniature golf, or boating. If you've always spent money on dates, include some dates that cost little or nothing, such as picnicking, bicycling, hiking, or taking some children to a park. Take your date to church. Pray with your date. Discuss the meaning of Scripture.

In short, let dating mature you, not restrict you.

3. *Identify love.* If we are going to "fall in love" first and then get married, and if dating is a process by which we discover whether or not we love that person, then it is important to be able to identify love as we date.

In pre-marital counseling, I'll always ask a couple why they want to marry. I've never had a couple say, "Because we can't stand each other. In fact, we hate each other so we thought we'd just get married." Couples have always answered, "Because we love each other." I will then ask, "How do you know you love each other?" Silence! Then a sort of blank look appears. I get the feeling each one is saying on the inside, "How *do* I know I love that person?" Love has to be more than a feeling. A feeling has a way of sprouting wings when the weather goes sour or when we eat the wrong thing.

A couple will usually say, "We know we love each other because we like to do things together." Isn't that nice? I have a dog, named Ginger. I love to do things with Ginger, but I've never thought of proposing. How about, "We get along so well"? I get along well with my mother-in-law. But marriage? Never! How about, "We have the same personality." But so do identical twins. Is that what you want—an identical sister or brother? Heaven forbid!

Well, if all of that is not love, what is love? More specifically, what is the kind of love to marry on? If we are going to get married because we love, then we need to have the kind of love and be loved with the kind of love that can keep us married, not just get us married. *Any* kind of love can get us married. But only one kind can keep us both married and fulfilled in it.

It is while you are dating that you need to ask, "What kind of love do I really have for this person, and what kind of love does he have for me?" There are three different kinds of love to evaluate:

A. *Eros love.* This is always one-way love—back to self. It's the "look out for number one" love. It's the "I love you *if* or *as long as* I'm getting my way." Does he always have to go to his favorite places and do his favorite things? Is there give and take? Do tempers rise often? Do you hear the line, "If you love me, you'll let me . . ."? That's *eros* love. And selfish *eros* love will never keep people together "for better or for worse."

B. *Philos love.* This is always a two-way love. It is a friendship love. Think of your closest friends. That's friendship love. It is a delightful and needed love. But it isn't the love to marry on. Friendship love demands that both "friends" are putting something into the hopper and drawing out of the hopper. As soon as one is no longer contributing meaningfully, we get new friends. We will still like that former friend, but the relationship has changed. This is the "I love you because of. . . ." There is a mutual cause that has attracted two people to each other and keeps them related to each other. It may be appearance: "I love you (friendship style) because you are beautiful or handsome." It may be abilities: "I love you because you are athletic, and I like to do athletic things."

But that casual kind of love is easily replaceable. Haven't you noticed that people can lose their "becauses"? What happens to the love "because you look great" when a Mack truck hits her in the face? What happens to that love "because you are athletic" when he gets a leg amputated?

Not only do we sometimes lose our becauses, but other people can come along with what may appear to be better becauses. "I thought *she* was beautiful, but that new girl who just moved in makes her look like a cousin to Frankenstein." Or, "I thought he was athletic, but this guy is headed for the Olympics." The "just because" kind of love has a way of changing too often.

C. *Agape love.* This is a one-way love. But it is always for the other person's well being. It sees a need in the other person and moves to meet it without counting the cost or calculating what's in it for number one. Agape love doesn't love what that other person can do for me or just one aspect of that person (such as looks or abilities), but loves the *total* person.

This is the only kind of love that can exist through both the good times and the bad times. How can it be identified during those dating days? By checking out the characteristics of this kind of love as listed in 1 Corinthians 13:4-7. If those kind of characteristics are normally missing, then it isn't *agape* love that is going on.

Here are some practical ways to check out this kind of love: (1) Once or twice meet him for a date dressed to go, but from the shoulder up looking and smelling the way you normally look and smell at 3:00 AM. If you have your hair in all kinds of funny looking contraptions, then meet him like that. You may discover soon that he loves a part of you, but not *all* of you. (2) Before setting the wedding date, spend at least two weeks living at his home with him and all the family members present, and then have him return the visit to your home. Two weeks at each place is the minimum. Most people can put up a front for a week. That's one reason we're so glad to see company leave— "Now we can be ourselves again." But not many people can pretend for two weeks in their own homes. By the end of the second week, notice how he treats every family member. (If your fiance lives alone, arrange frequent and concentrated times with his closest friends with whom he wears no masks.) Notice what irritates him. That will give you strong clues about what you will be living with. And don't think, "That person will be different in *our* house." You will marry him as he is, and he may stay that way for a long, long time. A person cannot adequately evaluate how well things will go in a marriage by just how well they go on the date. On that date, you can drop her off at the house or dorm when you've had a little argument. And if it's been *eros* love or *philos* love, you may decide not to date again. But in marriage, he/she does not drop off at another place. She comes into the same house as you do. And the argument may continue. In fact, it probably will.

The Teenager and Sex

We are living in a sex-saturated world. Teenagers are pressured by their peers to act like adults. They are pressured by music, movies, literature, and commercials. Some teenage movie stars have become sex symbols before they were old enough to get a driver's license. Because of their own body changes, teenagers are very aware of sexual feelings. At one time, their sexuality was sort of a Rip Van Winkle awaiting to be awakened. But during the teens, that sleeping becomes a wide-awake, active dynamo inside of them. And when that dynamo is daily exposed to the lure of sex that is beamed to the teenagers from every corner, it's like pouring gasoline onto a fire.

The teenager must decide to control this powerful force that lies within him. The sexual dynamo is not just a switch for crawling into bed. It is a center of power that affects the whole person—not just certain parts of his body. The sexual dynamo produces impetus for developing creativity, personality, emotions, energy, motivation, relational dimensions, maturity, and commitment. To flaunt sex as just a means to be satisfied physically for a time is to reduce its potential for benefiting the total person. It is to reduce the self to the level of animal passion only. It is to be a human who lives with barnyard ethics. In the barnyard, animals engage in sex with no love, no plans, no responsibility, and no follow-up care. Their sex is for a physical fling only. But not so with humans. Sex is for the whole individual, not just for intercourse. In fact, for humans, sex refers to the total self. Everything a human does is sexually related. I am male from the top of my head to the bottom of my feet. My sexuality is not part of me, but *all* of me. I speak as a *male,* sleep as a *male,* and laugh as a *male.* I am a total human person, not just a sex organ walking around. Consequently, I must allow my brains to remain above my shoulders, not below my waist.

Because sex refers to the whole person and affects the whole person, it is essential that we hear what God has to say about it. And God has some definite things to say, because He loves us. The physical act of sexual intercourse must be under control lest we allow one aspect of us to dominate and thus prevent our total self from developing in a good balance. For instance, a teenager who jumps out of one bed into another will discover that he is not allowing the sexual dynamo inside of him to help him develop meaningful interpersonal relationships, commitment, or stability. He will discover that such a one-sided expression of sex will hamper the emotions—the sensitivity to care, to laugh, to cry. Those emotions may get out of balance. A person may laugh too much without the capacity to be serious and to weep when others weep.

This is not suggesting that every time a person has some dimensions out of balance, the reason lies in an adequate understanding, control, and expression of his sexual dynamo. But it *is* suggesting that the sexual dynamo is one of those powerful influences that can affect our holistic balance if not controlled. In fact, any one aspect of our total self that gets out of control can affect the balance of the total self.

What is the primary Biblical control for sex? There are two: (1) Within marriage; (2) Done with *agape* love within marriage. Sexual activities within marriage, expressed with *agape* love, can help the social, psychological, physical, and spiritual health of the total person. That's why God commands abstinence from sexual intercourse outside of marriage (1 Thessalonians 4:3-8) and commands sexual activity within marriage (1 Corinthians 7:1-5). (See chapter 4 for the various benefits for sexual activity within marriage.)

The unmarried teenager should carefully study 1 Thessalonians 4:3-8. Here are some highlights of that passage:

Verse 3: "For this is the will of God, your sanctification; that is, that you abstain from sexual immorality." Do you want to know God's will? One aspect of His will deals with your sex life before marriage. He wants your sanctification. That means to be "set apart." He wants you to be different. How? By abstaining from sexual immorality. The Greek word for sexual immorality here is again *porne*. It refers to any sexual activity forbidden by God—incest, homosexuality, and intercourse before marriage. To be "set apart" with your sex life also means that you have set yourself apart *from* others in physical sexual activities so you can be set apart *to* your mates when you marry.

Verse 4: "That each of you know how to possess his own vessel in sanctificiation and honor." "To possess his own vessel" can refer to two things: (1) *Possess* can mean *take* and *vessel* can refer to a wife. Paul may be saying that a man needs to take his wife in sanctifiction and honor. That means that he so conducts himself that he brings her to the altar as a virgin. (2) This phrase may also mean to control his sexual organ. Either way, the end result is the same—no sex before marriage.

Verse 5: "Not in lustful passion, like the Gentiles who do not know God." Don't let the passionate emotions control you. That's the way the world lives. But the Christian is in Christ and has unconditional power in Him—the Holy Spirit. And the Holy Spirit gives the power for self control. "For God has not given us a spirit of timidity, but of power and love and discipline" (2 Timothy 1:7).

Verse 6: "And that no man transgress and defraud his brother in the matter because the Lord is the avenger in all these things, just as we also told you before and solemnly warned you." We transgress and defraud a brother when we engage in sex before marriage by taking something we had no right to take—the virginity of another. When a person has intercourse with a virgin, he has taken something that can never be replaced. The breaking of the hymen is irreversible. The woman will not be exactly the same again. It's unlike any other expression of love (or exploitation). Only that person's husband or wife has *that* privilege of the celebration of sharing virginity breaking. So we steal something from them ahead of time. The girl who gives herself to a man before marriage has also defrauded her potential husband. The Greek word for "defraud" means to cheat someone out of something. It's the word for greed, which literally means to reach out after something beyond which you should. Sex before marriage is not just fornication, but also stealing, greed, and covetousness. No wonder it affects the total self. It openly disobeys many commands of God.

Verse 7: "For God has not called us for the purpose of impurity, but in sanctification." Live the life God has called us to, not the life the culture lures us to. God does not give us privileges without responsibilities. Sexual rights with another demand personal commitments that go beyond the bedroom, but into lifelong developments within marriage. What is terribly wrong with the physical love act of becoming one flesh outside marriage is that it is not preceded by a cleaving relationship. While the sex act can be a "one flesh" act for the moment, when it is devoid of leaving mother and father and cleaving to a mate, it is sin. Notice the elimination of leaving and cleaving in 1 Corinthians 6:16, 17: "Or do you not know that the one who joins himself to a harlot is one body with her? For He says, 'The two will become one flesh.' But the one who joins himself to the Lord is one spirit with Him." That's the reason it is called immorality (1 Corinthians 6:18).

Verse 8: "Consequently, he who rejects this is not rejecting man but the God who gives His Holy Spirit to you." That's serious. It isn't the "kick up your heels and have a ball" that the world makes it out to be.

But how can a teenager resist temptation? Resisting temptation that tugs at us is never easy, because we are tempted by our desires. We desire it. But desire is not wrong. Solomon's advice to his son can still help any teenager:

1. Sexual sin is pleasant (Proverbs 9:17). Solomon didn't try to cover up the fact that the act can be pleasurable. Parents don't help by ignoring realities.

2. Sexual sin is damaging (Proverbs 9:18). Solomon talked about long-range consequences, not just short-range fun. That's what the world doesn't tell us.

3. Sexual sin is often related to a series of things. So be on guard when these are present—loneliness, revealing clothing, sweet sensual talk, secrecy, flirting eyes, and suggestive touching (Proverbs 7:5-23).

As a wise father, Solomon explained to his son what kinds of persuasions can reduce our resistance and entice us. Solomon's son was then better able to understand what was happening and to stop it.

Here are some positive steps a teenager can take:

1. Establish close family ties.

2. Discuss desires, temptation, and situations with parents.

3. Establish close fellowship with church people.
4. Control your thoughts.
5. Stay away from bad situations.
6. Be active in service projects—doing things for others.
7. Be energetic in a variety of interests—sports, church, school.
8. Don't envy the popular people.
9. Think purity.
10. Think about giving your virginity to your mate during the honeymoon.
11. Love self.
12. Remember that God will not permit anyone to be tempted above his spiritual ability to resist, and God always provides a way to escape (1 Corinthians 10:13).

If you have engaged in pre-marital sex, don't panic. Confess it to God, turn away from it—NOW. God's grace is greater than a person's disgrace. He's in the forgiving business. He's our Father who is not trying to get even. But He does couple His forgiveness of the repentant person with a command, "Neither do I condemn you; go your way. From now on sin no more" (John 8:11).

For Your Consideration or Discussion

1. Discuss the question of whether the Western practice of "dating" is to be preferred to the Eastern practice of arranged marriages.
2. If dating is to be done, what do you think is the earliest age for it to be allowed by parents?
3. Who is more responsible for controlling sexual stimulation (petting) on a date, the girl or the boy?
4. How would you respond to this statement: "Sexual intercourse between two unmarried persons is not sinful if they love each other and are committed to each other." Do you agree or disagree? State your reasons.
5. Do you agree or disagree with the following statement: "Petting to orgasm is not as immoral as sexual intercourse itself." Discuss it. What about petting short of orgasm?

Chapter 6

INCEST AND PORNOGRAPHY

Incest

Nearly 100,000 cases of incest are being reported each year. What makes that figure even more shocking than it appears is the fact that incest is often not reported. How many situations are not reported? Nearly one-third of the cases that are reported involve children under six years of age. V.D. of the throat in children under one year old is now being discovered.

The acceptance and encouragement of incest is coming from pornographic material that both depicts incestuous acts and includes erotic literature describing sexual activities between members of the same family. Some pornographic literature includes letters from the readers who discuss incest as a favorable practice. There is probably a direct correlation between the broadening exposure of pornographic material and the apparent increase of incest.

However, we cannot put all the blame on the pornographic material. Some movies and television programs have recently included incestuous activities without condenmation. A recent article published by the Sex Information and Education Council of the United States entitled, "Dealing with the Last Taboo," says that laws against incest in the U.S. are too harsh. The thesis of the article is that the taboo against incest is mindless prejudice—it's one of the primitive ideas that ought to be discarded. The article says such things as: (1) Incest has nothing to do with sexually perverse behavior; (2) Incest is an "obviously appropriate behavior" in some "healthy situations"; (3) Incest is a "sophisticated life-style"; (4) Drum beating against incest is damaging even to those not involved in incest; (5) The prohibition against incest helps some parent-child relationships to deteriorate because some parents are so afraid of incest that they totally withdraw affection from their children. The article suggests that we should abolish incest laws except in cases of rape and child abuse.

Time magazine cited numerous other examples of what it called the incest "lobby." A John Hopkins researcher said, "A childhood sexual experience such as being the partner of a relative need not affect the child adversely." A professor at Tufts said, "Children have a right to express themselves sexually, even with members of their own family." A University of Utah professor said, "It is questionable if the cost (of the incest taboo) in guilt and uneasy distancing between intimates is necessary or desirable." The co-author of the original Kinsey Report said, "It is time to admit, among other things, that incest between children and adults can sometimes be beneficial."

Another source that encourages incest is the child rights movement, which maintains that discrimination due to age differences should be outlawed. Supporters of the child rights movement say that a child should have the right to have sexual activities with whomever he wishes.

All of the above "lobbyists" for eliminating the laws against incest are positively fed by many contemporary sex researchers who teach that all forms of sex are good as long as the participants are consenting. That means anything is good as long as people want to engage in it. The Christian must reject that philosophy without hesitation. When God says something is not good, it is not good, whether or not we understand the reasons. God understands us so well. He knows the psychological, social, mental, and spiritual benefits or injury that practices offer to people. With that in mind—for our good—he has both positive and prohibitive commands for us.

Incest is not new. It's been around since as early as Lot (Genesis 19:30-38). However, God issued strict commands against it. He forbade sex between children and their parents (Leviticus 18:7), brother and sister (Leviticus 18:9), stepbrothers and sisters (Leviticus 18:11), step-parents and step-children (Leviticus 18:17), grandparents and grandchildren (Leviticus 18:10), in-laws (Leviticus 18:15; 20:12, 14, 20,

69

21), nephews/neices and their aunts or uncles (Leviticus 18:12-14).

Incest brought God's curse upon the guilty (Deuteronomy 27:20-23). God never diluted His command against incest. Centuries after His commands were communicated to the people of Israel, He cited incest as one of the rebellious sinful activities of Israel (Ezekiel 22:10, 11). Incest had infiltrated the membership of the church at Corinth (1 Corinthians 5:1). The church had overlooked its seriousness (1 Corinthians 5:2), but Paul hadn't (1 Corinthians 5:3). He called for the church to excommunicate the offender (1 Corinthians 5:5). This strict action was taken to prevent the practice from spreading (1 Corinthians 5:6, 7) and to bring the sinful person to repentance. The behavior in his life—the "works of the flesh" kind of behavior—needed to change. That's what Paul meant by saying, "For the destruction of the flesh" (1 Corinthians 5:5). The disciplinary action of the church was effective, for the person did repent (2 Corinthians 2:6-8).

Biblically, incest is sin, but the guilty can be forgiven if they repent and turn from it. God is not in the business of locking us up into our past sins. Our sorrow because of sin can bring salvation because of the Savior.

I now rejoice, not that you were made sorrowful, but that you were made sorrowful to the point of repentance; for you were made sorrowful according to the will of God, in order that you might not suffer loss in anything through us. For the sorrow that is according to the will of God produces a repentance without regret, leading to salvation; but the sorrow of the world produces death. For behold what earnestness this very thing, this godly sorrow, has produced in you: what vindication of yourselves, what indignation, what fear, what longing, what zeal, what avenging of wrong! In everything you demonstrated yourselves to be innocent in the matter (2 Corinthians 7:9-11).

Pornography

The word *pornography* comes from two Greek words that mean writing *(graphe)* about perverted sex acts *(porneia)*. The word *obscene* comes from a Latin word whose root means filth. Pornography has been found in both written and pictorial form on the walls of caves that date back to antiquity. It is not a new phenomenon. However, pornography is coming out of the closet in this country. In 1957, the Supreme Court ruled that obscenity is not within the Constitutional protection of the freedom of speech and press and that nudity is not obscene. Since 1957, the porno industry has mushroomed. Today, the porno industry has nearly 15 million regular subscribers to porno magazines, plus the over-the-counter sales. In 1968, a Presidential Commission on obscenity and pornography recommended to the President and to Congress that all laws of any kinds prohibiting pornography be eliminated. Neither the President nor Congress acted upon that recommendation.

However, the laws governing obscenity are vague. The vagueness begins with the definition. What is offensive to one person or to a certain community may not be offensive to another person or to another community. What offends sexually has some cultural and temporal dimensions to it. For instance, at one time the exposure of a woman's ankles was sexually offensive in this country, but not today. In some cultures, the exposure of a woman's face is sexually offensive, but not in this country. In this country, the exposure of a woman's breats in public is offensive to most, but not in many African countries. Some friends of mine were serving on a mission field where bare-breasted women was the norm. As soon as some of the women were converted to Christ, the missionaries gave them blouses to wear. Those women hadn't been home long wearing their blouses when their husbands came to the missionary's house with fierce anger. In that culture, the only women who wore blouses were prostitutes. These husbands did not like the social stigma the missionaries had given to their wives. Those missionaries also learned that drinking a certain juice for breakfast (which they commonly drank in the United States) was sexually offensive.

It is difficult to outlaw obscenity if it can't be defined. And that's part of our difficulty today. The current law determines obscenity by three guidelines: (1) The dominant theme of the material taken as a whole must appeal to the purient interest in sex. That means it appeals to physical sexual arousal by inciting lustful thoughts. But that varies with people, communities, and time. (2) The material affronts contemporary community standards relating to the description or representation of sexual matters. But who decides what the community standards are? Is the community a neighborhood, city, county, state, what? (3) The material is utterly without redeeming social value. But who decides that? The subjectivity of those three criteria have allowed the porno industry to continue and grow with few restriction. The courts have had a difficult time putting teeth into banning pornography since criteria for determining what is obscene cannot be objectively interpreted.

In trying to tighten up the criteria, Judge Harlan said that an obscene work must consist of "debasing portrayals of sex" and be patently offensive. But "patently offensive" was not defined. A contemporary writer, Harry Clor, has been a tremendous help in emphasizing that the obscene dehumanizes and depersonalizes the human. He wrote that pornography is "sexual obscenity in which the debasement of the human element is heavily accentuated, is depicted in great physiological detail, and is carried very far toward its utmost logical conclusion." Clor's more elaborate definition follows:

An obscene book, story, magazine, motion picture, or play is one which tends predominantly to:
1. Arouse lust or appeal to prurient interests.
2. Arouse sexual passion in connection with scenes of extreme violence, cruelty, or brutality.
3. Visually portray in detail, or graphically describe in lurid detail, the violent physical destruction, torture, or dismemberment of a human being, provided this is done to exploit morbid or shameful interest in these matters and not for genuine scientific, educational, or artistic purposes.
4. Visually portray, or graphically describe in lurid physical detail, the death or the dead body of a human being, provided this is done to exploit morbid or shameful interest in these matters and not for genuine scientific, educational, or artistic purposes.
(Harry M. Clor, *Obscenity and Public Morality: Censorship in a Liberal Society*, Chicago: University of Chicago Press, 1969, p. 245.)

Although Clor has a tighter handle on defining obscenity, his definition is not the one followed by the courts. Therefore, we are left adrift concerning a very important and serious social issue; and as long as we stay adrift, the people of the porno industry will be laughing all the way to the bank.

It's Not That Innocent

Some people may ask, "Why the fuss? This is a free country, isn't it?" Yes, it is, but freedom is not the license to do whatever we please at the expense of others and at the detriment of a community and a country.

Pornography just is not the innocent industry that some would like us to believe it is. Studies have revealed that over one half of the police chiefs in this country believe that pornography contributes to juvenile delinquency. Studies also reveal that masturbation increases, sexual conversation increases, rape increases, teenage pre-marital intercourse increases, and deviant sexual behavior increases after exposure to explicit sexual literature and scenes. One study, which interviewed prisoners who were serving time for sex crimes, revealed that 38% of such prisoners admitted that being exposed to pornography was a contributing factor to their sex crimes. The prisoners surveyed said that they wanted to try the various sexual activities shown by pornography and that 38% of the prisoners went out and did try what they saw.

What did they see? Pornography is not just about sex between a man and a woman. It includes incest at all levels, sex with animals, homosexuality, the sex-torture of children, the torture of women after sex acts, and gruesome scenes of murder and violence.

In fact, UPI reported that some porno movies show AC-TUAL murders done on the set. Females in at least eight films were actually knifed to death after sex acts and their bodies were ACTUALLY dismembered on film. These women did not know that these were to be their last films.

In 1973, the Houston, Texas, police department dug up the bodies of twenty-two teenage boys who had been sexually abused and murdered by sex-torture devices sold in pornography shops. The two murderers lived out the kind of murder they had been taught via porno movies.

J. Edgar Hoover once wrote, "I believe pornography is a major source of sex violence. I believe that if we eliminate the distribution of such items, we shall greatly reduce our frightening crime rate" (Neil Gallagher, *How to Stop the Porno Plague*, Bethany Fellowship, 1977, page 19). The report of the Commission on Obscenity and Pornography supported Hoover's statement. With documentary testimony, the Commission reported the committing of chilling crimes by people who saw them done in porno films. A *Readers' Digest* article, "Sultan of Smut," stated, "The pornography trade has been marked consistently by ganglandstyle violence. Police records in several states reveal a pattern of strong-arm tactics directed at those connected with smut" (November, 1975, pages 107, 108).

An investigation by the *New York Times* found that mafia money and members are heavily involved in porno. The Criminal District Attorney in San Antonio, Texas, conducted an intensive investigation through a special Grand Jury and concluded that organzied crime is behind porno in the southwestern states. That Grand Jury discovered that approximately 90% of porno in the U.S. is controlled by only three groups, which operate in cooperation with the national crime syndicate. Porno financially supports crime.

Pornography treats women like things and pawns, not like people worthy of respect. It plants into the fabric of our society anti-women ideas. It cheapens women by putting them on display like some commodity. It suggests that women are good for only one reason—a sexual plaything to be treated any way a man wants. It suggests that woman's only value is the pleasure she can give to the whims and selfish physical pleasures of a man. It suggests that women are mindless. If for no other reason, the women in a community should campaign against pornography because of what it does to womanhood. Testimonies reveal that many women in porno are lured into drugs and then forced into porno to keep up the drug habit. In fact, they are lured into drugs for the purpose of abusing them in porno. Pimps for organized crime stalk the bus depots at major cities looking for lovely girls away from home who are low on money.

Pornography is filled with unbelievable scenes of violence, crime, child abuse, brutality, and torture. One magazine that is openly displayed and sold in most communities depicted a full-page color cartoon of a man seducing a doll-clutching, pig-tailed little girl. It also included a naked Jesus on the cross with a Roman soldier performing sodomy on Jesus, as well as a naked nun and the Pope (in color-cartoon) fondling each other. Using little children in pornography is out of control. Police report that many missing children have probably been picked up and used in the porno industry.

The Gallup and Harris Polls show that 80% of the people in the U.S. oppose pornography. It is not easy to do, but it is essential for Christians to take a stand against pornography. An adult bookstore was *legally* closed because people opposed it. Neil Gallagher has written an important book that deserves study and implementation—*How to Stop the Porno Plague*, (Bethany Fellowship, 1977).

The Bible and Pornography

Does the Bible have anything to say against pornography? Yes! First of all, in an indirect way, the Bible lists many wholesome purposes for sex (see chapter 4). But pornography disregards all of those and reduces sex to physical self-satisfaction of an exploiter motivated by lust only. It dehumanizes that life which was created in the image of God. The Bible also condemns the exposure of nakedness outside marriage (Leviticus 18:6-18). Jesus taught against looking upon a woman for the purpose of lusting after her (Matthew 5:27-30). To tear out the eye or cut off the hand was an Aramaic way of saying, "Get rid of the situation that motivates lust." Pornography is the "right eye" and "right hand" of many people. It is interesting that Jesus spoke against situations that cause lust just before His teaching about divorce (Matthew 5:31, 32). That was surely intentional. Pornography, which feeds on lust, surely weakens a husband and wife's commitment to each other. And that's the reason Jesus spoke about sticking to vows immediately after the divorce teaching (Matthew 5:33-37). Notice the relational regression. Situations that feed lust (and pornography certainly does) can weaken a husband and wife's *agape* love for each other. The weakening of that bond can cause either one or both to disregard their verbal vows to each other *because* pornography weakens their "one flesh" physical vow to each other. As pornography weakens a husband and wife's physical bond with each other, it helps violate Biblical teaching that a man should rejoice in his wife, be captivated by her love and be satisfied with her breasts (Proverbs 5:18-20). A person may begin to look at pornography as an "innocent" curiosity seeker. He may be completely satisfied with his mate. But pornography itself is not that innocent. It can gradually raise questions about the mate. She doesn't look *that* great or act *that* way in bed. The difference between the porno queen and the wife gradually weakens the marital commitment, which violates the marital vows. Pornography is like a cancer. It can start so minutely, but eventually it pollutes the total life of a person. There is no allowable place for it in the homes or private lives of God's people.

Pornography is surely included in applying in the twentieth century some of the apostolic teachings of the first century. (Remember the word *porneia* is the source of our word *porno;* so pornography is certainly included, though not exclusively, in the following references.)

> Abstain from . . . *porneia;* if you keep yourselves free from such things, you will do well . . . (Acts 15:29).

> Flee *porneia.* Every other sin that a man commits is outside the body, but the *porneia* man sins against his own body. Or do you not know that your body is a temple of the Holy Spirit who is in you, whom you have from God, and that you are not your own? For you have been bought with a price: Therefore, glorify God in your body (1 Corinthians 6:18-20).

> And just as they did not see fit to acknowledge God any longer, God gave them over to a depraved mind, to do those things which are not proper, being filled with all unrighteousness, wickedness, greed, evil, full of envy, murder, strife, deceit, malice . . . (Romans 1:28, 29). *(It's interesting that all of these descriptions are in porno films.)*

> Now the deeds of the flesh are evident, which are: *porneia,* impunity, sensuality . . . (Galatians 5:19).

> But do not let *porneia* . . . even be named among you, as is proper among saints (Ephesians 5:3).

> Set your mind on the things above, not on the things that are on earth (Colossians 3:2).

> Therefore consider the members of your earthly body as dead to *porneia* . . . (Colossians 3:5).

> Food is for the stomach and the stomach for food; but God will

do away with both of them. Yet the body is not for *porneia*, but for the Lord; and the Lord is for the body (1 Corinthians 6:13).

For this is the will of God . . . that you abstain from *porneia* (1 Thessalonians 4:3).

Abstain from every form [or appearance] of evil (1 Thessalonians 5:22).

Now flee from youthful lusts, and pursue righteousness, faith, love and peace . . . (2 Timothy 2:22).

Do not love the world, nor the things in the world. If anyone loves the world, the love of the Father is not in him. For all that is in the world, the lust of the flesh and the tsst of the eyes and the boastful pride of life, is not from the Father, but is from the world. And the world is passing away, and also its lusts; but the one who does the will of God abides forever (1 John 2:15-17).

There was *porneia* in the city of Corinth, and it had affected some in the church. Paul wrote for the Christians to repent of it, "I am afraid that when I come again my God may humiliate me before you, and I may mourn over many of those who have sinned in the past and not repented of the impurity, *porneia* and sensuality which they have practiced" (2 Corinthians 12:21).

If Paul felt he might mourn over some of them, how about some of us? It's one thing for Paul to make a drop-in visit and discover that some had not repented of *porneia*, but it's another thing if Jesus at His second coming discovers people who have not repented of *porneia*. It could result in being excluded from Heaven, for outside the gates of Heaven will be those who practiced *porneia* without repentance (Revelation 22:15).

Pornography always affects the mind first. Consequently, Paul's advice is as necessary for us today as it was for the Philippians in his day:

Finally, brethren, whatever is true, whatever is honorable, whatever is right, whatever is pure, whatever is lovely, whatever is of good repute, if there is any excellence and if anything worthy of praise, let your mind dwell on these things. The things you have learned and received and heard and seen in me, practice these things; and the God of peace shall be with you (Philippians 4:8, 9).

For Your Consideration or Discussion

1. Why do you suppose that the courts and American society as a whole have never been able to agree on a definition of obscenity or pornography?
2. Do you agree with Harry Clor's definitions of pornography?
3. Do you agree that there is a cause-effect relationship between pornography and incest? Between pornography and sexual crimes?
4. Do you believe it is legally possible for communities to close porno shops if they want to?
5. What, in your opinion, is the fundamental cause of interest in pornography? Discuss it.
6. If you are studying this book with a group, ask a Christian attorney to meet with your group to discuss the legal aspects of attempting to close porno shops.

Chapter 7

WHAT GOD WANTS
FOR MARRIAGE

God stated His intentions about the purpose and character of a marriage in Genesis 2:18 ("It is not good for the man to be alone; I will make a helper suitable for him") and 2:24 ("For this cause a man shall leave his father and his mother, and shall cleave to his wife; and they shall become one flesh"). He also made it clear that He wanted marriage to be permanent.

The Need for Marriage

Genesis 2:18 is the foundational verse showing the need for marriage. God designed man to need a mate. The male and female were to live as helpers for each other. They were not only to live *with* each other, but they were to live *for* each other. Solitude is a form of helplessness; thus, God made male and female for each other. But interdependence calls for commitment in a relationship. Just putting two people together to meet each other's needs does not insure interdependence. So God designed marriage.

Marriage is the commitment relationship that provides the environment where interdependence can happen. Marriage is a covenant relationship (Malachi 2:14) in which two people commit themselves to help one another. It is because of this interdependence between wife and husband and because it can only be lived out in a covenant relationship, that God said, "For this cause a man shall leave his father and his mother, and shall cleave to his wife: and they shall become one flesh" (Genesis 2:24).

The Character of Marriage

While Genesis 2:18 is the foundational verse showing the

need for marriage, Genesis 2:24 is the foundational verse showing the *character* of marriage. That is the reason Jesus always quoted Genesis 2:24 when He was asked about divorce (Matthew 19:5; Mark 10:7). While people asked Jesus about the time span of a marriage, Jesus spoke about the character of a marriage. To be uncommited to the character of a marriage is to put ourselves outside of God's intentions for our fulfillment and happiness.

God intends the character of a marriage to involve (1) leaving father and mother, (2) cleaving to the mate, and (3) becoming one flesh. This is the kind of relationship God wants to exist in a marriage; this is God's plan for men's and women's happiness and completeness.

• *Leaving*

Marriage involves the loosening of one human relationship (parent-child) in order to tighten another. This initial surrender of security and protection provided by each mate's parents should continue to characterize the yielding of both mates throughout the whole of the marriage. That is why we read in the New Testament that the husband should give himself up for his wife (Ephesians 5:25). As children with our parents, we are basically self-oriented; when we become married, we should become other oriented.

• *Cleaving.*

Second, marriage involves the sharing of one total person with another total person. Basically, the word *cleaving* means "a joining." But the implications are stronger. It is a word used to mean the opposite of withdrawing from a person (2 Kings 18:6). It means a determined and devoted persistence to stay with a person (Ruth 1:14). It describes a stick-to-itiveness, a gluing or cementing together (Ezekiel 29:4; Job 19:20; Psalm 22:15; 119:31; Jeremiah 13:11). It involves giving praise, loving (Deuteronomy 11:22; 30:20; Joshua 22:5), respecting, and serving (Deuteronomy 10:20). A cleaving relationship is basic to forming a community—a common oneness. The Greek equivalent is sometimes used in the New Testament to describe one who adopts the objectives of another (Luke 15:15).

• *One flesh*

This phrase spotlights the physical consummation of marriage in the sexual act, but that's not all. It also denotes a powerful communion in which two people, through leaving and cleaving, are sharing a oneness in purpose and goals as seen in the word picture, "yoke." To be one is to be yoked together as a team (*joined* in Matthew 19:6 is the word *yoked*).

Two people's mere "living together" does not constitute a marriage. Too many people want to bypass the leaving and the cleaving and simply engage in the sexual aspects of the "one flesh" dimension. By doing so, they pervert what God intended marriage to be. There needs to be a cementing and a covenant making recognized by the community in order for there to be a marriage in God's eyes.

Every action and reaction in a marriage should be measured by whether or not that action or reaction is performing or perverting the leaving, cleaving, one-flesh relationship. When Abraham ignored his wife by saying she was his sister, he violated all three aspects of the interpersonal relationship that God intended. Instead of leaving a situation of security, he ran to protection and left his wife. Instead of cleaving to his wife, he cut her off. Instead of them acting as a team, he acted as a lone ranger. He disregarded his covenant relationship with her.

What should happen to a marriage when a husband acts like that? Sarah provides us with the model. She did not run off to the Reno, Nevada, of her day to get a divorce. She manifested the love that is described in 1 Corinthians 13:4-7. She displayed long-suffering, and her marriage was saved. And what blessings came out of that union!

The Permanency of Marriage

When Jesus was asked about divorce, He stated God's intentions by referring to the creation of male and female: "Have you not read, that He who created them from the beginning made them male and female, and said, 'For this cause a man shall leave his father and mother and shall cleave to his wife; and the two shall become one flesh'?" (Matthew 19:4, 5). He connected the permanency of marriage to that plan when He said, "Consequently they are no more two, but one flesh. What therefore God has joined together, let no man separate" (19:6).

Jesus teaches us two significant things: He reminds us when a marriage takes place in the mind of God, and He tells us how long that relationship is expected to last. A marriage exists when a leaving, cleaving, and a one-flesh relationship is in force. A marriage continues when both mates are committed to cutting loose from their parent-child relationship and making a covenant that they will be permanently committed to their sexually consummated relationship. In fact, the word for marriage *(gameo)* means to fit together, to pair together. The word itself stresses a life shared between two.

Termination of Marriage
Any termination of a marriage except by natural death is a departure from God's original intention. However, because of the situations sin brought into the world, God did allow marriage to be dissolved for other reasons.

In the Old Testament, there are two categories of marriage terminations: (1) execution of one of the mates, and (2) divorce. In both cases remarriage was allowed.

● *Termination by Execution*
Before the giving of the law on Mt. Sinai, sexual infidelity was punishable by death (Genesis 38:24). It is interesting to note that Tamar was a widow, but she had been promised to a man (38:11). That promise carried with it the same commitment as marriage did—a commitment to fidelity.

Later, punishment for sexual perversions was developed in detail. Punishable by death were such perversions as incest (Leviticus 20:11), sex with an in-law (20:12, 14), homosexuality (20:13), and sex with animals (20:15, 16); topping the list was sexual infidelity of a married person (20:10).

"If a man is found lying with a married woman, then both of them shall die" (Deuteronomy 22:22)—a rather permanent way to end a marriage. Why was sexual infidelity punished so severely? Because it tears apart the covenant relationship. It destroys the intimacy of the "one flesh." It is impossible to be one with your mate if you are sexually intimate with another person.

Paul drew a graphic picture of this destruction when he wrote, "Or do you not know that the one who joins himself to a harlot is one body with her? For he says, 'The two will become one flesh' " (1 Corinthians 6:16). This certainly does not mean that the two people who engaged in sex had a marriage relationship; there was no leaving and cleaving involved. This type of sex is immorality. That is the reason Paul wrote, "Flee immorality" (6:18), soon after the above statement. Sexual infidelity can so seriously threaten the interpersonal commitment that God intended for a husband and wife that it could permanently dissolve a marriage.

When a marriage is shattered, devastating pollution is poured into society. Children are hurt, and a whole generation with different value systems is born. So God decided to stop that pollution by the execution of those who participated in that type of immorality.

- *Termination by Divorce*

God also permitted divorce: "When a man takes a wife and marries her, and it happens that she finds no favor in his eyes because he has found some indecency in her, and he writes her a certificate of divorce and puts it in her hand and sends her out from his house . . ." (Deuteronomy 24:1). The big question is—what is the indecency?

By Jesus' day, two main interpretations were given by Jewish scholars. The followers of Shammai believed that indecency referred to adultery only. That view had little support because Moses had just outlined the action to be taken with adultery—death. The verse in Deuteronomy 24 was a continuation of Moses' speech.

The followers of Hillel believed that indecency referred to anything the husband did not like in his wife, such as talking with a man in public, wearing the hair down over the shoulders, talking too loudly, burning the food, or not looking as nice as other women.

While "adultery" was too narrow an interpretation, "anything" was too broad. The Hebrew word for "indecency" is used thirty-nine times elsewhere in the Old Testament. It is not restricted to sexual intercourse, but it usually does refer to some shameful sex acts. The word literally means "nakedness or exposure of a thing." (Note its usage in Genesis 9:22, 23; 42:9-12, Exodus 28:42; Leviticus 18:6, 17; 20:11; 1 Samuel 20:30; Isaiah 20:4; 47:3; Lamentations 1:8; Ezekiel 16:8, 36, 37; Hosea 2:9).

Indecency (in Deuteronomy 24:1) probably originally referred to rebellion against the husband, particularly the wife's nakedness and sexual perversion with another person just short of intercourse. However, in Jesus' day, most Jews interpreted indecency to mean anything the husband did not like about his wife.

It is important to note that Moses did not command the divorce (only the bill of divorcement) as he had the death. Why? Jesus said in Matthew 19:8, "Because of your hardness of heart, Moses permitted you to divorce your wives; but from the beginning it has not been this way."

Many people hitchhike on the fact that Jesus used the word "permit." It is pointed out that the Pharisees in verse 7 asked, "Why then did Moses command . . . ?" But Jesus changed the word *command* to *permit,* suggesting that this was something allowed but not necessary. However, in Mark 10:3-5, it is Jesus who uses the word *command* and the Pharisees who use the word *permit.* Thus, the two words seem to have been interchangeable in Jesus' day.

Some suggest that the bill of divorcement was Moses' doing, not God's; but that cannot be supported. Moses was recording God's instruction, as seen in the beginning of Deuteronomy: "And it came about in the fortieth year, on the first day of the eleventh month, that Moses spoke to the children of Israel, according to all that the Lord had commanded him to give to them" (Deuteronomy 1:3). This was God's teaching, to which not one word was to be added or deleted (Deuteronomy 4:2). Deuteronomy 24 is part of that instruction; Moses was not adding or subtracting from God's Word, and Jesus was not suggesting that he did.

Why, then, did God command through Moses that a bill of divorcement be given? Evidently the men were dismissing their wives without such a bill. This action put the wife in an unbearable state. She needed her husband for survival; but when he put her out, she was without protection. Neither was she free to marry again. In order to make a living, she might turn to harlotry, which would constitute committing adultery against her husband. Then the husband could apply the death penalty to her. Moses (and God) guarded against that kind of heartless action.

The bill of divorcement was a legal dissolvement in the

eyes of the community; it permitted remarriage. Without such a bill, remarriage was not permitted. God would not have commanded the bill if He did not recognize the remarriage; the purpose of the bill was to allow remarriage for the sake of the women. Moses assumed the woman would remarry another: "And she leaves his house and goes and becomes another man's wife, and if the latter husband turns against her . . ." (Deuteronomy 24:2, 3). Notice that she became another's wife, and he was called her husband. Her first husband was hers no longer; she began a new relationship. The bill of divorcement dissolved the first relationship.

The bill of divorcement read something like this:

On _____ day of the week, _____ day of the month _____ in the year_____ I_____ who am also called son of_____ of the city of_____ by the river of_____ do hereby consent with my own will being under no restraint, and I do hereby release, send away, and put aside thee, my wife _____ who is also called daughter of_____ who is this day in the city of_____ by the river of_____ who has been my wife for some time past; and thus I do release thee, and send thee away and put thee aside that thou mayest have permission and control over thyself to go to be married to any man that thou mayest desire; and that no man shall hinder thee from this day forward, and thou art permitted to any man, and this shall be unto thee from me a bill of dismissal, a document of release and a letter of freedom, according to the law of Moses and Israel.

_____ son of_____ witness
_____ son of_____ witness*

Although a divorced person as well as a widow could remarry, neither could marry a priest, for he was to marry only a virgin (Leviticus 21:14). The divorcee's second marriage was not considered an adulterous situation. But if after that second marriage, she went back to her first husband, God would consider that an abomination. "Her former husband who sent her away is not allowed to take her again to be his wife, since she has been defiled (meaning she had consummated a new union); for that is an abomination before the Lord" (Deuteronomy 24:4). This prevention of remarriage between former mates was to keep the men from play-

*Jewish Encyclopedia. Printed by permission of Ktav Publishing House, New York, New York.

ing games with their wives and from making rash decisions. Once he divorced her, he was to remain divorced from her forever.

There were two situations in which a man was clearly prohibited from divorcing: when the husband falsely charged the wife with infidelity (Deuteronomy 22:13-19), and if a man had sex with an unengaged virgin (and was discovered). He would have to marry her and was not allowed to divorce her ever (Deuteronomy 22:28, 29). An interesting way to curb premarital sex—don't you agree? These rules protected the women from being shamed and then rejected.

Conclusion

From the beginning, God has intended for marriage to be a lifelong commitment to a covenant relationship. This covenant is sealed by both partners' *leaving, cleaving,* and becoming *one flesh.*

However, there are situations and actions that prevent these three intended aspects of the marriage relationship from functioning as God wishes. In those cases, when the covenant relationship is shattered, God allows the marriage to be dissolved. We will take a closer look at those situations in the next chapters.

For Your Consideration or Discussion

1. Can a couple have a good marriage without the leaving, cleaving, one-flesh aspects intact? Why or why not? Are these aspects single events or developing processes? Or some of both? Discuss.
2. Staton says, "Every action and reaction should be measured by whether or not that action or reaction is performing or perverting the leaving, cleaving, one-flesh relationship." Do you agree? If so, how can this be done?
3. The controversial subject of divorce is introduced in this chapter. Check the following statements with which you agree. Discuss.
    a. Emotions are stronger on this subject than on most other topics. _____

b. The Bible does not give clear instructions on the ethics of divorce and remarriage. _____

c. The Bible does not cover all of the possible "grounds" for divorce. _____

d. Jesus did not intend to give a complete discussion on divorce, but confined himself to the single question, "May a man divorce his wife for any and every reason?" (NIV). _____

e. Many of the arguments about divorce go beyond what the Scriptures actually say. _____

f. The church lacks compassion. _____

g. The church does not take seriously its own doctrine of sin. If it did, it would not be surprised or shocked that people do divorce. _____

Chapter 8

WHAT THE BIBLE TEACHES ABOUT DIVORCE

The church is not exempt. Just watch all those hands go up in any group of Christians when you ask, "How many of you have experienced a divorce yourself or in your immediate family (parents, brothers, sisters, or children)?"

Indeed, divorce is one of the major issues in our society. More than one million couples will go through a divorce this year. And it is getting easier to do. "No fault" divorces have been adopted by forty-seven states. California has put the "mail-order" divorce into effect. This is the no-lawyers, no-courts, no-legal-hassles divorce. Childless couples who have been married less than two years can apply for this divorce, which will automatically be granted by mail six months later. The couple decides on the settlement between themselves. More than a dozen other states are studying this California creation; it is expected to spread nationwide.

The church is concerned and rightly so. Just where does divorce place a person in his relationship to God? And the questioning becomes even more urgent when remarriage is being considered. This is probably the toughest practical problem facing the church today.

We can approach the problem from at least three different angles: (1) the society approach—go along with the times and change when society changes; (2) the Biblical approach—practice the principles of the Bible; (3) the individualistic approach—ignore both society and the Bible, and do "your own thing."

"Do not love the world, nor the things in the world" (1 John 2:15) cautions us against the society approach. "If any . . . wishes to come after Me, let him deny himself" (Matthew 16:24) cautions us against the individualistic approach. "Long for the pure milk of the word" (1 Peter 2:2) points us to the Biblical approach.

Yet the Biblical approach is not as easy as it sounds, for there are at least six ways to study the Bible on any topic such as divorce.

(1) Isolation: Finding and quoting one verse and developing your entire understanding from it, regardless of context. One example would be to quote Luke 16:18 ("Everyone who divorces his wife and marries another commits adultery, and he who marries one divorced from a husband commits adultery") and let it rule every situation.

(2) Traditional: Letting the way you have always believed dictate the answer. It is the idea of, "Don't confuse me with the facts; I've already made up my mind."

(3) Inner feeling: Reading a passage and understanding it on the basis of what "I feel" it means.

(4) Proof text: Stringing together several verses that support one line of thought—the line of thought that you have already made up your mind to support.

(5) Cultural: Suggesting that the Biblical teaching about divorce and remarriage applies to only the culture for which it was first written.

(6) Holistic: Attempting to study everything the Bible says about divorce and remarriage, taking into consideration the context, the culture, and the original meaning of the words. This kind of study allows you to come to a conclusion different from what you originally thought. This latter approach will be the one that I will use. Get ready to dig *into* the Word with me, and be ready to dig *out* of your preset ideas. The only way the Bible can be our guide is by allowing *it* to direct *us*, and not vice versa. We do not want to master it; we want it to master us!

(A CAUTION: We will not all agree about the meaning of some of the texts, but our differences should not in any way jeopardize our kinship to each other in Christ. He is the essential who unites us to the Father and to each other. God's family has always consisted of people who did not agree at every point, as it shall always be. I seriously doubt that this study will find universal acceptance among God's people, but the test is in how we treat each other.)

Hated, but Forgiven

Although God allowed marriage to be terminated for other reasons than by natural death, these terminations were departures from God's original intention for marriage. Marriage was created for the welfare of the male and female, but that purpose cannot be fulfilled in temporary interpersonal relationships. From the beginning, God intended marriage to be permanent so that its purpose could be realized.

In principle, marriage is a lifelong commitment to live out a covenant relationship. Divorce is a breach of that covenant. Even when permitted, it is still an act of treachery that God hates (Malachi 2:14, 16).

But this does not mean that God will not forgive divorce. The Hebrew word *hate* is used in many other places in the Old Testament to spotlight things God detests; yet God is willing to forgive what He hates. God also hated Esau (Malachi 1:3), the misuse of feast days (Amos 5:21), robbery for burnt offerings (Isaiah 61:8), idolatry (Jeremiah 44:4), all who do iniquity (Psalm 5:5), and those who love violence (Psalm 11:5). Each of these situations violate God's original intentions; that is why He hates them. Such actions pervert the ideal life God had in mind for men, but none of these is unforgivable.

God understands the pain of divorce. He uses the metaphor of divorce to describe His own severed relationship with Israel (Jeremiah 3:8). He himself was deeply grieved by the shattering of that covenant relationship. But when Israel repented, He welcomed her back. Past failures were forgotten, and a new day had dawned.

A new day has dawned for us, too. When we have God's indwelling Spirit within us, we can forgive rather than fracture. We can enjoy a new life of love and peace in Jesus. It is no wonder that Jesus had some quite revolutionary thoughts about divorce.

What Jesus Teaches

By the time Jesus began teaching, divorce and remarriage had become the popular thing to do. In fact, being divorced and remarried many times was more the norm than the exception. The historian Seneca records that people got married in order to get divorced and got divorced in order to marry again. People recalled the years in the past not by the names of the emperors, but by the names of their wives or husbands of those years. He told of one woman who had been divorced and remarried twenty-five times, and she was her present husband's twenty-third wife.

Many of the people in Jesus' crowds had been divorced and remarried. Jesus' teaching on the subject was quite revolutionary; so revolutionary that at the end of His most detailed teaching, His disciples responded, "If the relationship of the man with his wife is like this, it is better not to marry" (Matthew 19:10).

Jesus both eased up and tightened down the two categories of marriage termination in the Old Testament. He eased up the dissolvement by death commanded in Deuteronomy 22:22, "If a man is found lying with a married woman, then both of them shall die" (see also Leviticus 20:10). Instead of favoring execution, Jesus said the guilty ones could be divorced (Matthew 5:31, 32). Not once did He command or even suggest that a person should be killed for committing adultery.

- *Remembered and Repeated*

In an indirect way, He even erased this command for execution entirely. Although John 8:1-11 may not have been in the original writing of John, it must record a genuine event in the life of Jesus, remembered and repeated by the people. The Jewish leaders tried to force Jesus to implement the death sentence. There was no guesswork involved; they had caught a woman in the very act of adultery (8:4). They had probably staked out the local motel purposely to trap her. They must have felt quite pious when their plan worked.

"Now in the Law Moses commanded us to stone such women; what then do You say?" (8:5). Not only did they trap the woman, they hoped to trap Jesus, also. If He did not go along with Moses' law, He would be disobedient. If He said "stone her," He would have acted beyond the current Roman law. However, the leaders were the ones who got trapped.

Jesus was not bound by the law, for it was a tutor to point people to Him (Galatians 3:24, 25). Now that He was on earth, He had the final word; He spoke only what the

Father, who gave the law in the first place, told Him to speak (John 12:49).

Instead of answering their question, Jesus began to write on the ground (John 8:6). We do not know what He wrote, but I suspect that what He wrote related to the fact that the woman was unfaithful to the marriage covenant and also related to the sins of others in the crowd.

He may have written Deuteronomy 24:1 ("When a man takes a wife and marries her and . . . he has found some indecency in her . . . he writes her a certificate of divorce") on the ground. The scribes and Pharisees knew they had been too liberal with their understanding of that verse. They described "indecency" as anything that did not please the husband—from burning the food to spinning around in the street. They were expecting to force Jesus into a literal interpretation of Deuteronomy 22:22, when they knew they were not interpreting 24:1 literally.

Then Jesus said, "He who is without sin among you, let him be the first to throw a stone at her" (John 8:7). After reading what Jesus had written, they began to realize that they, too, had been acting treacherously.

Jesus stooped down and wrote on the ground the second time. The crowd grew very still and began to walk away one by one, beginning with the oldest (8:9). What could He have written the second time that caused an angry crowd to disperse in silence? He might have spelled out on the ground the shameful sexual acts that the original word "indecency" meant. The men would have been self-condemned, knowing how they had perverted God's Word and how many divorces they had been responsible for. Jesus might also have written Malachi 2:16, " 'I hate divorce,' says the Lord."

I do know that Jesus did not do things without related purposes. Whatever He wrote must have caused the accusers to face their own sins. They were defused by a quick reminder of how they had distorted God's intentions for marriage.

- *Released for a Reason*
  We can find Jesus' direct teaching on divorce in Matthew 5:31, 32; 19:1-12; Mark 10:1-12; and Luke 16:18.

The Greek word for divorce means a release (freedom). It means a total dissolving; it is the opposite of being bound.

This same word was used to describe the freedom given to Barabbas (Mark 15:6, 9, 11, 15), the total dissolving of debt (Matthew 18:27), the release from a disease (Luke 13:12), and the release from life itself *(depart* in Luke 2:29). Under the law, a divorce allowed those involved to remarry without sin.

The Jews had been saying a man could divorce for *any* reason, but Jesus allowed divorce for only *one* reason. That word *(porneia)* has been translated "unchastity" (Matthew 5:32), "adultery" (Matthew 19:9), "marital unfaithfulness," "fornication," and "unfaithfulness."

Some suggest that the word means intercourse between unmarried persons—fornication. Others suggest it means adultery—sexual intercourse between a married person with anyone besides the mate. However, the word *porneia* is not restricted to either of those meanings. It really means "perversion," which includes such sins as sodomy, incest, homosexuality, adultery, and beastiality. The word itself does not tell us the kind of sexual perversion, just the fact of it. See its use in 1 Corinthians 10:8 (cf. Numbers 25:1, 2); 1 Corinthians 5:1, 11; 6:13, 18; 1 Thessalonians 4:3; Colossians 3:5; Ephesians 5:3-5; Galatians 5:19; Revelation 2:20, 21; Acts 15:20, 29). Probably the best translation of this word would be simply "sexual immorality."

Except for the reason of sexual immorality, if a man divorced his wife, he shared the responsibility of her committing adultery when she married another. In the days of Jesus, women had very few other options than to remarry in order to avoid poverty. Also, the man who married her would commit adultery, as well as the husband who released her if he married again (Matthew 19:9).

But how could the woman and her new husband be charged with adultery and the former husband who married again be so charged, if divorce totally dissolved the covenant relationship in a marriage? Jesus was saying that not *every* kind of divorce dissolved a marriage from God's perspective. Jesus was not going along with the "divorce for any reason" practice. Sexual immorality was the only valid reason for issuing a bill of divorcement. Illegitimate divorce (for a reason other than sexual immorality) would not dissolve a marriage; the couple were still bound to each other.

Jesus' teaching was revolutionary and tough for men to live with, but it was primarily to protect the women from mistreatment by their husbands and the resulting stigma placed upon them. Jesus erased the double standard that had been practiced for years.

But what happened if a couple divorced because of sexual perversion? That divorce would dissolve the marriage, and they would be free to remarry. That remarriage would not be an adulterous situation (that is why the word "except" is in the verses). The divorce and remarriage still violate God's original intention ("from the beginning it has not been this way," Matthew 19:8), but they are allowed.

It is true that Mark 10:12 and Luke 16:18 do not have the "except" clause, but that does not eliminate it from Jesus' teaching. Not to include it in a couple of places is not to cancel it everywhere else.

- *Remarriage and Repentance*

The problem facing us today is this: What if we have already been divorced and remarried for a cause other than sexual immorality?

Jesus did not address himself directly to this problem. His teaching was designed to curb the wholesale divorce for any cause that was so common in His day. But most of His audience would have been divorced and remarried. Jesus did not condemn them in their present state, nor did He tell them that they were living in a continual state of adultery. Neither did He tell them to return to their first mates. The situation of meeting the woman at the well (John 4) gave Jesus the ideal opportunity to say all of the above thoughts, but He didn't.

When the woman told Jesus she had no husband, Jesus replied, "You have well said, 'I have no husband'; for you have had five husbands; and the one whom you now have is not your husband" (4:17, 18). Jesus did not say, "You have had one husband and have been living in adultery ever since." He did not even say, "Wrong. You do have a husband, your first. You are still married to him. Go back to him." Jesus evidently recognized her previous divorces and remarriages, but He did not recognize her living with a man as being in a marital state.

It is possible that she had been widowed five times; but in

light of the popular custom of divorce and remarriage, that does not seem likely. It is also possible that she had been divorced five times for the right reason (sexual immorality on the part of her husbands), but that is doubtful; men did most of the divorcing, not the women. I believe she had been divorced and remarried five times; each man was called her husband except for the one with whom she was presently living.

Why didn't Jesus condemn her for her divorces? Wasn't she living in adultery ever since that first divorce? I doubt it. The New Testament does not clearly state that a person is continuously living in a state of adultery after an illegitimate divorce. It is possible that only the initial act of remarrying constitutes adultery. It is possible that the initial act of adultery committed by remarrying severs the covenant relationship; then the new union is considered a marriage. Although it began in an adulterous encounter, it may not remain so. Jesus never said that remarried people were living in continuous sin; that has been the conclusion of men. If remarriage constituted continuous adultery, I suspect He would have clearly stated it. Living in a continuous state of adultery would be living in continuous unrepented sinfulness. The children would be technically illegitimate, and the church would have a case for exercising the kind of discipline applied in 1 Corinthians 5. But whichever way you understand the adulterous situation, we must not forget that God is a forgiving God.

God has never made it a practice to accept only those people who have made perfect decisions in the past. Jesus did not condemn that woman at the well or tell her to return to her first husband, but this does not mean He was approving of her actions. Neither was He locking her up into the past. Instead, He was giving her hope for her future and demonstrating for us what God does in such situations. Her future indeed became much brighter, and she led a city-wide revival.

It is hard for many people to accept the grace of God with relation to divorce and remarriage. Many will think that I am saying that God approves of divorce and remarriage. Many will think, "Well, if God is like that, then anyone can get a divorce and remarry—God will forgive."

The mature Christian does not seek loopholes to take advantage of God's grace. The Christian understands that unrighteousness hurts God. He also understands that God's kindness toward us is not designed to encourage us to repeat our sins, but rather to lead us to repentance (Romans 2:4). Of course, some may take advantage of God's forgiveness, but that will not cancel God's grace. We must not deny God's grace to all just because some misuse it.

Divorce and remarriage is not what God wants in His creation, nor what we want in our country. But let's face it. Divorce and remarriage are what we have! We must teach in such a way as to slow down the trend; yet we need to minister to those many people who are hurting because of the pain of divorce and to those who feel they may be lost because of it. Let's reach out to both with God's truth and God's grace.

What Paul Teaches

In his teaching about divorce, Paul followed in the footprints of both Moses and Jesus. They all explained something old by recording God's original intentions for remarriage and something new by listing allowable exceptions. The chart on page 98 shows how.

Paul did not want the allowable exception he would introduce to erase the knowledge of God's original intentions for marriage; so he introduced and concluded his discussion of the exception with God's original wishes.

• *God's Original Intention*

In Romans 7:2, Paul repeats what Moses allowed for the dissolvement of marriage, the natural death of a mate: "For the married woman is bound by law to her husband while he is living; but if her husband dies, she is released from the law concerning the husband." Then, in verse 3, he repeats what Jesus said: "So then if, while her husband is living, she is joined to another man, she shall be called an adulteress." Paul is making it clear that couples should stay married. Of course, this does not mean that the "except" clause that Jesus used (except for sexual immorality) would be canceled by Paul's silence about it.

The situation that Paul is discussing in 1 Corinthians 7 concerns Christians who were married to Christians and

96

also mixed marriages between Christians and non-Christians. Evidently sexual immorality was not an issue.

In verses 10 and 11, Paul is reaffirming God's original intentions for marriage: "But to the married I give instructions, not I, but the Lord, that the wife should not leave her husband (but if she does leave, let her remain unmarried, or else be reconciled to her husband), and that the husband should not send his wife away." That was just another way of saying, "What therefore God has joined together, let no man separate" (Jesus' words in Matthew 19:6).

● *A New Exception*

In verses 12-16, Paul introduces a new exception. Some suggest that Paul went beyond Jesus' teaching. Paul does say, "But to the rest I say, not the Lord" (v. 12). What did he mean by that? Most people think (and I agree) that Paul was simply saying that Jesus did not himself talk about this exception during His earthly ministry. But that does not mean Jesus would not agree with Paul's conclusion. Paul was an apostle of Jesus (1 Corinthians 1:1). He was on Jesus' mission with Jesus' message. Paul taught what he received through revelation (Galatians 1:12). It would be against Paul's nature to cancel or go beyond what Jesus taught.

Then why didn't Jesus include this exception in His ministry? The answer is obvious. Jesus spoke about situations His audience encountered; there were no Christian/non-Christian marriages then. But in Paul's time, many Christians were married to non-Christians, and it was about them that Paul was speaking.

Paul affirms that the Christian should seek to carry out God's original intentions. In 1 Corinthians 7, he was telling the Christian not to initiate, suggest, or encourage the dissolvement of the marriage. The unbelieving mate would be sanctified through his believing mate (v. 14). This does not mean he is necessarily set apart to the Lord; it means the unbelievers' commitment to the marriage is enhanced by the believer's conduct. The marriage can remain a legitimate marriage in the eyes of both mates and God.

"Yet if the unbelieving one leaves, let him leave; the brother or the sister is not under bondage in such cases" (v. 15). What does "is not under bondage" mean? It is not the same Greek word that is used in 1 Corinthians 7:39: "A wife is bound as long as her husband lives." Thus some suggest that the mates would still be legally bound (as husband and wife in the eyes of God) but not functionally bound. They would not have to live out the marriage responsibilities (and privileges), but they would still be married. This interpretation has some merit, because the word for "is under bondage" in verse 15 is the word for service (douloo), while the word for "bound" in verse 39 is the word that stresses the actual connection of things joined together (deo). However, these two words are used interchangeably elsewhere in the New Testament in discussing a person's relationship to the law (Romans 7:1, 2; 8:15; Galatians 4:9). It seems to me, then, that they are also used interchangeably in 1 Corinthians 7.

If one is not bound to the law, he is totally freed from it to belong to another (Romans 7:4); and if a person is not bound (same word) to an unbeliever who leaves (1 Corinthians 7:15), that person is also totally free to belong to another.

Paul emphasizes this thought again when he says, "Are you bound to a wife? Do not seek to be released. Are you released from a wife? Do not seek a wife. But if you should marry, you have not sinned" (7:27, 28). The person who is released in released indeed.

	God's Original Intention	Allowable Exceptions
Moses	Genesis 2:24	Leviticus 20:10 Deuteronomy 22:22 Deuteronomy 24:1-4
Jesus	Matthew 19:3-8 Luke 16:18; Mark 10:2-12	Matthew 19:9 Matthew 5:32
Paul	Romans 7:2, 3 1 Corinthians 7:10, 11 1 Corinthians 7:39	1 Corinthians 7:12-16

Paul listed two ways in which a person is released from marriage in this chapter: By natural death and by the action of an unbelieving mate who initiates the release. Beyond this, Paul said nothing about divorce and remarriage.

Most of Paul's audience would have had experience with divorce and remarriage. The Romans even had a law that divorcees had to marry within eighteen months after the dissolvement of a marriage to avoid a special tax. While divorce and remarriage was certainly not preferable to God, Moses, Jesus, or Paul, it was a reality—as it is today.

• *God's Grace*

What should we do when people are divorced for other reasons than those allowed in the Scriptures and then want to remarry? We should first emphasize God's original intentions for marriage and try to curb the ever-rising divorce rate. Yet we must realize that many will not wish to remain unmarried. The basic drives of sexuality are still alive and crave to be fulfilled. Children desire and need to have both a mother and a father figure in the home.

A divorce shatters so much. Needs abound. People hurt. Loneliness mounts. Let us not withhold the truth that Jesus promised to receive *all* who come to Him (Matthew 11:28; John 6:37), including those who divorce and remarry.

What about Christians who divorce and remarry? It is easy to condemn them, but we must remember the inclusiveness of God's forgiveness (1 John 1:9). Christians who err need to be admonished; they need to repent. They also need to be loved by God's family. We are all on different levels of spiritual growth; yet we are brothers and sisters who need each other and need to help each other.

So a brother or sister divorces and remarries. Do we kick them out of the family? Or do we minister to them with the heart of God? I suggest we do the latter.

Emphasizing God's grace is not opening the door to license. It is opening the door for Christians to commit themselves to live in accordance with God's intentions. Paul said it well in Romans 5:20—6:2:

> But where sin increased, grace abounded all the more, that, as sin reigned in death, even so grace might reign through righteousness to eternal life through Jesus Christ our Lord. What shall we say then? Are we to continue in sin that grace may increase? May it never be! How shall we who died to sin still live in it?

God does not approve of divorce; yet He is willing to work around it. Just think of all the things He endured in the Old Testament! Polygamy was certainly not God's intention, but He put up with it and used some of those polygamists as His vessels. Consider Jacob, David, and Solomon, for example.

Let us couple truth with love (agape) and encourage a multitude of sinners to be daily transformed into the likeness of Jesus. Let us not deny that privilege to those who have committed sins of immaturity.

For Your Consideration or Discussion

1. Jesus said, "I tell you, anyone who divorces his wife [except for marital unfaithfulness], causes her to commit adultery, and anyone who marries a woman so divorced commits adultery." The phrase in brackets is the so-called "exception clause." Do you think that Jesus would also make exceptions for the following behavior?
   Wife beating: Agree _____ Disagree _____
   Severe alcoholism: Agree _____ Disagree _____
   Spouse's refusal to work, although able to do so:
   Agree _____ Disagree _____
   Spouse's incest with one or more of the children:
   Agree _____ Disagree _____
   Spouse joins a religious cult and is gone for 2 or more years: Agree _____ Disagree _____
   Spouse becomes an atheist and insists the spouse and children not attend church:
   Agree _____ Disgree _____

2. 1 Corinthians 7:27, 28 in the King James Bible reads: "Art thou bound unto a wife? seek not to be loosed. Art thou loosed from a wife? seek not a wife. But and if thou marry, thou hast not sinned." Since this version is a literal translation from the Greek and since the word "loosed" is the same word used for divorce, do you think Paul is saying that, although he prefers that divorced persons not remarry, if they do, they have not sinned"? Discuss it.

Chapter 9

THE CHURCH AND DIVORCE—
WHAT NOW?

In the previous chapters, we have considered closely the Biblical teaching about divorce and remarriage. Although the Bible does not extensively deal with the subject, two emphases come through clearly: (1) God's intentions for marriage, and (2) certain exceptions that God allows because of man's situation. The Bible gives us both foundational truth for a successful marriage and functional grace when failures arise. The functional grace comes from the heart of our Father, who does not lock a person into his past failures. Nevertheless, those failures grieve the Father; He does not want His grace to be used as an excuse for viewing failures lightly.

So what does the church do today when people continue to violate God's intentions for marriage and allowances for divorce? Several different possible attitudes may determine our reactions. You will probably be able to find your past and present reactions in the following list:

• *The "locked-in" attitude.* In this approach, the church treats those who were unscripturally divorced and remarried as if they are eternally locked into their past failures. It is the belief that unless they abandon their present marriages, they are lost. They are living in a continual state of sin. Their children in the second marriage are technically considered illegitimate. A minister who uses this approach will often refuse to counsel with anyone thinking about remarrying after a divorce. He certainly will not marry them.

To implement this approach consistently, the couples in question should be disassociated from the church. However, not many churches do that officially. Instead, they do it personally—by looking down on the couple and their family, by shying away from them, and by not allowing them to get involved in the work of the church. As far as the church is concerned, they no longer have abilities that can be used for the Lord; they will no longer make any contribution to the family of God. They are not allowed to teach, to work with the youth, to help with the music program, or to do benevolent work. If they want to use their abilities in unselfish avenues, they will have to go to the Red Cross, volunteer to the local hospital, or help with community projects outside the church.

These people are looked upon as having committed the unpardonable sin as long as their first mates are alive. They would be sooner forgiven if they had murdered their first mates instead of divorcing them.

• The "as if it never happened" attitude. This approach ignores the situation. The "marrying parson" models this attitude—if you want to get married, just knock on his door! The church with this attitude would never have an all-night prayer meeting for a member about to go through a divorce. A divorce is thought of as "just one of those things." Any hurt that is involved is overlooked. Divorce is "winked at"; thus, divorces multiply—sometimes among Christian leaders.

• The revelational and redemptive attitude. With this approach, the church offers help and service. The church will continue to uphold God's intentions for marriage without allowing current situations to stifle the teaching of God's Word about the permanence of marriage. At the same time the church will also offer a redemptive service for those whose marriages have failed, showing them the true character of God by forgiving and loving them. "All the paths of the Lord are loving-kindness and truth" (Psalm 25:10; see also 40:10, 11; 85:10; 89:14; Proverbs 3:3; 14:22; John 1:14). This latter approach is what I consider to be the most helpful and the most pleasing to God.

Telling the Truth

Our children grow up with many erroneous ideas about marriage. Here are a few of them: (1) Marriage will solve all my problems. (2) If I get married, I will never be lonely again. (3) By marriage I can escape my parents. (4) Marriage is like an eternal date. (5) I will change him/her after we are married. (6) In marriage, our differences won't cause trouble. (7) Marriage is a trap or prison. (8) Marriage takes all the fun out of life. (9) Marriage is simply a legal piece of paper.

The church and the home must unite to tell the truth about marriage to young people *before* they get married. We must do more to prepare people for marriage. We need to teach the function for marriage and the permanence that God intended for marriage. We need to teach the realities and the practicalities of the relationship and to erase the fantasies.

The church can help by offering special clinics and retreats for engaged couples and by teaching Biblical guidelines for marriage in the youth groups. The church can decide to take Paul seriously by having the older women teach the younger women about marriage (Titus 2:3-5).

The church can also offer classes exposing the futility of divorce. Divorce is often not helpful, but hopeless. This is one of the reasons God hates it. He knows us and wants only what is good for us. Divorce is not a cure-all. Divorce is not what it is cracked up to be. To think that divorce is going to produce instant bliss is wrong; it is about time people heard about the suffering and problems that inevitably accompany marriage breakups.

Divorce brings terrible trauma for both children and adults. The children feel cheated and forsaken. They feel guilty, wondering whether they are to blame. They want to love both parents, but they feel as if they are in a tug-of-war. The happiness of holidays is marred by trying to decide which parent to be with.

Statistics show that second marriages are not any happier than first marriages and have an even shorter life span. Aspirin cannot cure a brain tumor, and divorce cannot cure marriage problems; it only covers them up for a while.

Before a couple remarries, the church needs to spend many hours teaching them about the ingredients of a successful marriage. If a person enters a second marriage with the same erroneous ideas and habits he had in the first, another failure looms ahead. Don't think it could not happen again. Ninety percent of those who have experienced one divorce experience two.

The church is partly to blame. If divorced persons are made to feel like unforgiven sinners, then why should they hesitate to get a second divorce? Hell won't be any hotter with two divorces on the record. The church must actively seek to help make the second marriage a success.

Let's face it. Seldom is one mate *totally* innocent when a marriage is dissolved. Both people have contributed to the breakdown. Unless a person knows where he was wrong, admits it, repents of it, and changes, he will carry the weakness into the new marriage. Destructive interpersonal relationships will not hold a second marriage together any more than they did the first one.

Too many people get married for the romance of it and the desire for personal happiness. Both of those reasons are self oriented. Then, when one mate does not get his way, he thinks about severing the relationship. A marriage should be the result of the commitment of two people to one another, not to self. The love in a marriage should be the love expressed in 1 Corinthians 13:4-7. It is imperative that we tell the truth about both marriage and divorce.

Extending Grace

We are all failures in certain areas of our lives. I doubt that any of us claim to have reached perfection. We have been cleansed from sin, but we still live with it. With this in mind, we Christians must have open hearts and minds, and reach out in love to those who are hurting because of divorce. Having love *(agape)* means meeting another's needs unselfishly; those who have been touched by divorce have many needs and must face many difficulties.

• *Look to the future.* Jesus opened the door toward a new future for the woman at the well (John 4). He did not ignore her past, but neither did He allow it to determine her future. A person who ignores his past failures or is drowning in guilt will not look to the future with any hope or security. The church must help people admit their errors, accept responsibility for their mistakes, and repent of them. Only then can a person be open to the forgiveness of God. And only then can he live in a new marriage with a bright future ahead.

I do not mean by this we should never use the divorced leader in the work of the church. It would depend on the attitudes shown and on the individual situation. We must not conclude that divorce automatically calls for discipline. The reasons behind the divorce are important. We also must not conclude that divorce never calls for discipline. But all discipline must be done with redemption in mind.

• *The need to feel worthy.* Divorce can make all those involved feel a sense of failure; personal self-esteem can lower a great deal. We in the church need to remember that a person's failure in one area of life does not mean he will fail in all areas. We need to go out of our way to make the divorced feel they are still worthy human beings.

I know of one woman who moved in with her parents (her father was a preacher) after her divorce. She was an expert in working with children; so the church put her in charge of the ministry to children. What a blessing she has been to that church! I have never seen anyone handle children any better. What a tragedy it would have been if that church had felt "failure in one area means failure in all."

• *The need for friendship.* A divorced person experiences many changes in personal relationships—with the mate, with the children, with in-laws, with friends of the couple, with the church. Sometimes jobs or residences are changed. Often a homemaker has to find a job to make a living; many times she has never worked outside the home before.

I am sure some divorced people feel just like this description in Psalm 102:6, 7;

> I resemble a pelican of the wilderness;
> I have become like an owl of the waste places.
> I lie awake.
> I have become like a lonely bird on a housetop.

They feel forsaken, lonely, with no one around who cares. They wonder whether there is any hope at all. But God regards the prayer of the destitute (Psalm 102:17). He looks down "from His holy height . . . to hear the groaning of the prisoner; to set free those who were doomed to death" (Psalm 102:19, 20).

God is concerned about those who have been seriously uprooted and feel forsaken. His church should express similar concern by gathering the divorced into a loving fellowship. Communication lines should be kept open. The divorced person should be invited into the homes of other Christians. The church should consider beginning a ministry to single adults so they will feel a part of a group that eats together and has fun together. If a congregation is too small, it should join with other area congregations to minister effectively to needs.

• *The needs of the children.* While children are growing, they need input from both sexes to establish their identity and to feel good about their lives. With over one million children living with only one parent, it is time the church started to be more aware. The children's classes should be taught by male-female teams. Men in the church should create opportunities to spend time with children who don't live with their fathers. Likewise, Christian women should build a relationship with motherless children.

Children of couples who have been divorced and remarried should not be treated as second-rate by the church. The children are not to blame; why should they be punished? The worst way to punish a child is to attack his self-esteem by looking down on him or ignoring his needs.

• *Practical problems.* Besides all the emotional difficulties, divorced people face many practical problems. The woman may need help with handling business matters like budgeting, buying insurance, home repairs, auto repairs, buying a house and car, job hunting, and getting financial aid. A man may need to know about cooking, cleaning, laundry, and caring for children's sicknesses.

The church can help see that these needs are met. I suggest that there be a special committee whose job it is to look into these matters and see what the needs are in each situation. I suspect that the elders and deacons of the first-century churches would have seen that these needs were met. We cannot assume that these matters will be taken care of by "somebody."

What a Divorced Person Can Do
A divorced person should not expect all the initiative and effort to come from others. Here are some suggestions:

• *Do not bury your abilities.* If your congregation is determined not to use your abilities "officially," then use them "unofficially." Get involved. You don't have to be the "big cheese" or have the approval of the elders to give yourself away in service. Find someone who needs your help and give it. Anyone in the hospital? Anyone shut-in at home? Anyone need a babysitter? Anyone need a good, hot meal? Anyone need someone to shop for him? Anyone need to "get away" from the pressures of life by going to a concert or a play? Get involved in service for others.

• *Don't remain in a rut.* Develop your interests. Take a class. Join a club. Take a trip. Read a new book. Start a Bible club in your home for the neighborhood children. Visit the local nursing home. Redecorate your home and do all the work yourself. Get busy. Don't sit around feeling sorry for yourself.

• *Keep up your physical appearance.* Even though you think no one cares how you look, visit the beauty shop or barber shop regularly. Why not try a new hairstyle or a different set of frames for your glasses?

• *Be mindful of your attitude.* Don't fret about what other people think or let their reactions control your actions. Forgive your former mate. Don't be bitter or critical. Admit your faults, repent, and change. Accept God's forgiveness. Trust in God's love.

• *Keep morally pure.* It might be easy to use the divorce as an excuse to fail in other areas of life. Don't turn to drink, illicit sex, gambling, or cheap thrills to bury your guilt or bitterness. Remember, you are God's child; you can use this experience to mature into the likeness of Christ. Jesus has both glory and grace to share with you.

• *Don't jump into another marriage.* If you can't see what you contributed to the divorce and have not changed, don't marry anyone—yet.

But can a divorced or divorced/remarried person be used in any leadership capacity in the church? It is so easy to lock a person into his past, isn't it? But God doesn't do that. God requires that a man be the "husband of one wife" to be an elder or a deacon (1 Timothy 3:2; 3:12; Titus 1:6). But if that has to be unchanged throughout all his past, then so must all the other characteristics in those passages.

Surely God is willing to use people who have repented of the past, accepted God's forgiveness, and are living according to God's life-style in the present. After all, that's what life with God does. It continually changes us into Christlikeness. We should not overlook the Christlikeness in a person's present life because of situations in his past.

Summary

God's original intention is that marriage be terminated only by natural death. Through His Word, however, He has revealed two exceptions—sexual immorality and an unbeliever's departure. That is God's truth.

But God's grace sees the broken and fragmented people who have been hurt by the onslaught of sin. Sin hits, like a hammer on an anvil, with many different kinds of blows. One of those is divorce.

But the Spirit of God working through the people of God can bring healing to the hurting people. Let us be determined to implement the balance between truthful content and tender compassion.

For Your Consideration or Discussion

1. Look at the list of "erroneous ideas" about marriage found on page 102. Discuss the following questions: Did you believe any of these "myths" when you married? If people do believe in such "myths," what is their source? Do successful marriages have to go through a process of "demythologizing"? How is that done? What can the church do to "demythologize" marriage?
2. Is it *ever* true that one of the mates is innocent of the marital breakdown?
3. Is the church's attitude toward divorced persons changing? If so, why?
4. Should ministers preach at least once a year on such topics as "Divorce and Remarriage" or "Divorce and the Church"? If you were divorced, what would you want the minister to say?

Chapter 10

ALCOHOL

The use of alcoholic beverages is not restricted to any particular time or geography. People in all cultures throughout history have been acquainted with alcohol in one form or another. Soon after the flood, Noah planted a vineyard from which he made wine and got drunk (Genesis 9:20, 21). I doubt that Noah dreamed up the idea of wine while he was on that ark. Wine making and wine drinking had probably been around before Noah's day. Christianity is divided over the issue of whether to drink any kind of alcoholic beverage in any amount for any reason or not. Some Christian groups devote much of their energy toward teaching total abstinence. Some Christians evaluate the maturity level of other Christians by whether or not they drink. Some equate maturity with total abstinence. Others equate maturity with drinking—he has "come of age." Emotions on both sides of the issue run high—and so do traditions. If we aren't careful, we can confuse our traditions with God's truth and then step into doing what Jesus criticized, "teaching as doctrines the precepts of men" (Mark 7:7). As with any issue, it is paramount that we study what the Bible teaches. And, as much as possible, we must do it without our prejudiced glasses on so we do not ignore what doesn't fit "our" position.

The Bible and Prohibition

I wish the Bible commanded total abstinence (because of all the problems connected with alcohol), but it does not. In fact, the Bible sheds some interesting light on the subject that is rather embarrassing to read—it's too liberal for many of us. Here are some of the Biblical teachings:

• *The making of wine.* The making of wine was assumed and not condemned in the Old Testament (Judges 6:11). In fact, we read that God's people were commanded to tithe their wine (Deuteronomy 14:22, 23; 18:4). The making of wine was so much assumed that God compared Israel to a vineyard and said that God "hewed out a wine vat in it" (Isaiah 5:2). The only time the making of wine was condemned in the Bible was when it was made on the Sabbath (Nehemiah 13:15). The people of the Old Testament considered wine as a staple food along with bread, corn, and oil (Genesis 27:37; 1 Samuel 16:20; 2 Samuel 16:1; 1 Chronicles 12:40; Nehemiah 5:11; Job 1:13). Describing the scarcity of food included the scarcity of wine (Lamentations 2:12).

• *Wine as a blessing from God.* When Moses was giving God's Word to the Hebrew people before they entered the promised land, he promised that God would bless them with new wine if they obeyed God.

> Then it shall come about, because you listen to these judgments and keep and do them, that the Lord your God will keep with you His covenant and His lovingkindness which He swore to your forefathers. And He will love you and bless you and multiply you; He will also bless the fruit of your womb and the fruit of your ground, your grain and your new wine and your oil, the increase of your herd and the young of your flock, in the land which He swore to your forefathers to give you (Deuteronomy 7:12, 13).

In fact, God caused rain partly so wine could be gathered (Deuteronomy 11:14). While some suggest that this is not the kind of wine that could make a person drunk, evidence does not support that position. The same Hebrew word used in these passages *(tirosh)* is used elsewhere to describe injurious results (Hosea 4:11).

Long before Moses, God's people had connected the availability of wine with God's blessings. The blessing that Isaac gave to his son, Jacob, included, "Now may God give you the dew of heaven, and of the fatness of the earth, and an abundance of grain and new wine" (Genesis 27:28).

The idea that wine was a blessing from God continued throughout the Old Testament. When speaking about the new covenant that would bring a new era to God's people, Jeremiah referred to wine as "the bounty of the Lord":

Hear the word of the Lord, O nations, and declare in the coast-lands afar off, and say, "He who scattered Israel will gather him, and keep him as a shepherd keeps his flock." For the Lord has ransomed Jacob, and redeemed him from the hand of him who was stronger than he. And they shall come and shout for joy on the height of Zion, and they shall be radiant over the bounty of the Lord—over the grain, and the new wine, and the oil, and over the young of the flock and the herd; and their life shall be like a watered garden and they shall never languish again (Jeremiah 31:10-12).

• *Wine as an offering to God.* Wine was one of those commodities that God's people were to tithe (Deuteronomy 14:22, 23; 18:4). Wine was a regular part of the daily sacrifice (Exodus 29:40). Wine is listed along with grain, oil, the firstborn of the herd and flock, the first shearing of sheep. It is difficult to pull wine out of that list and declare it a "sin-drink" while the other items are morally clean. Wine was one of the products that God commanded be given by the community at large to the Levites, and singers, the gatekeepers, and the priests (Nehemiah 13:5, 10-13; Numbers 18:12). Was God commanding that sin be shared with them?

One of the special offerings that God commanded His people to present to God in the promised land included wine (Numbers 15:1-10; 28:14). While some suggest that this is not the wine that could cause someone to get drunk, evidence does not support that. The same Hebrew word for wine here *(yayin)* is used elsewhere to describe the wine that caused drunkenness (Genesis 9:21; 19:32; 2 Samuel 13:28; Esther 1:10).

• *Lack of wine as punishment from God.* While new wine was seen as a reward for honoring God (Proverbs 3:9, 10), the failure of wine was seen as evidence that people had sinned; so God was withholding His blessing (Jeremiah 48:32, 33; Hosea 2:9; 9:1, 2; Haggai 1:11). It was considered to be a tragedy for a man not be privileged to enjoy his wine and oil (Hosea 9:2; Joel 1:10).

• *Wine as a symbol.* Wine was Biblically used as a positive symbol for what God was doing. It was used to symbolize the new covenant era (Jeremiah 31:10-12; Isaiah 27:2). It was used to describe the productivity God desired in the new kingdom (Matthew 9:17). It was also used to describe joyous human experiences (Song of Solomon 1:2, 4; 4:10).

• *The gathering of wine as celebration.* One of the festival seasons that God commanded His people to observe was the Feast of Booths, to be observed after the people had "gathered in from your threshing floor and your wine vat" (Deuteronomy 16:13).

• *Wine as a gift to the needy.* When a Hebrew slave was set free, he was not to be sent away empty-handed. God commanded, "You shall furnish him liberally from your flock and from your threshing floor and from your wine vat; you shall give to him as the Lord your God has blessed you" (Deuteronomy 15:14).

• *Wine as a prescription.* Paul prescribed a little wine to Timothy to aid Timothy's stomach problems (1 Timothy 5:23). Perhaps Timothy had practiced total abstinence, but Paul suggested another avenue for Timothy's good. In the Old Testament, God gave wine to man to gladden man's heart (Psalm 104:14, 15), and a joyful heart is considered good medicine (Proverbs 17:22). It was given to those who were weak and faint in the wilderness (2 Samuel 16:2).

• *Abstinence as a special vow.* On occasion, some people would make a special vow of consecration to God called the Nazarite vow. This vow included the abstinence from wine, strong drink, grape juice, anything produced by the grape (including raisins), hair-cutting, and touching a dead body (Numbers 6:1-7). This was for a specified time—not a lifetime vow. While some suggest that Christians should follow that vow about drinking wine, they do not include such things as abstinence from raisins or the prohibition against a man's getting a haircut.

• *Jesus and wine.* On one occasion Jesus turned some water into wine at a wedding feast (John 2:1-11). Jesus admitted that He himself drank some wine in contrast to John the Baptist, who did not (Luke 7:33, 34). Jesus was accused by His enemies as being a gluttonous man and a drunkard (Luke 7:34). Although the charge was false, it would not even have been tried had it been common knowledge that Jesus practiced total abstinence from both eating food and drinking wine.

• *Two Categories of Wine in the New Testament?* Any

attempt to find two categories of wine in the New Testament—one intoxicating and one non-intoxicating—is futile. It is true that the wine used as a food item was two parts of wine to three parts of water. However, it is not true that that was non-intoxicating. When Jesus turned the water into wine, it was the diluted wine He made *(oinos)*. However, the steward of that banquet made it clear that the good wine that Jesus made had the capacity to make people drunk (John 2:10). Although *oinos* is that diluted wine, thus unlike much of our wine today, it had an alcoholic content and impact to it. It wasn't like our grape juice.

The Greek word that Paul prescribed for Timothy is the Greek work *oinos*. This was also used to describe the wine that can make a person addicted (1 Timothy 3:3; Titus 1:7), and can make a person drunk (Ephesians 5:18). In fact, two of the Greek words for a drunkard come from this same word *(oinoptes, oinophlugia)*. The charge of Jesus' being a drunkard comes from this Greek word. If *oinos* is just like our grape juice, then the charge of being an *"oinos-*bibber" would have been meaningless. If *oinos* is incapable of producing drunkenness, then what is the need to prohibit leaders in the church from being addicted to it (1 Timothy 3:3)? If *oinos* is always non-intoxicating, then why spotlight the fact that John the Baptist never drank it (Luke 1:15; 7:33)?

The Bible and Responsibility

While the Bible does not command total abstinence, neither does it condone irresponsibility. It was the production and use of wine as a *food* item that was permitted and even encouraged in the Old Testament. However, drinking wine just to be drinking wine as an *intoxicating beverage* was not encouraged. In fact, that kind of drinking was condemned. God warned against the dangers of alcohol as a drink of pleasure.

While the Bible permits wine drinking, it is also our best source for outlining the dangers of wine. It affects the mind by causing a person to forget important decisions (Proverbs 31:5) and to have hallucinations (Proverbs 23:33). It can cause a person to become insensitive to the needs of others (Proverbs 31:5). It can cause a person to perish (Proverbs 31:6), to get bitter (Proverbs 31:6), and to become unrealistic (Proverbs 31:7). Alcohol is a depressant, not a stimulant; so it can give a person a negative outlook on life (Proverbs 23:29, 30) or cause him to lose purpose and meaningfulness in living (Proverbs 23:35). It can take away understanding (Hosea 4:11) and make a person sick (Hosea 7:5). It can affect the way a person walks (Isaiah 28:7). It can affect a person's judgment and make him confused (Isaiah 28:7). It can make a person vomit (Isaiah 28:1-8). It can bring a person to poverty (Proverbs 21:17). It can take away a man's wisdom (Proverbs 20:1). It can betray a person (Habakkuk 2:5). It can destroy a man's home life (Habakkuk 2:5). It can become so addictive that a man is never satisfied—thus he becomes an alcoholic (Habakkuk 2:5).

If wine can do all of that, isn't that enough to command total abstinence? It may seem as if it is, but the fact is that God didn't any more command total abstinence from wine than did He command total abstinence from other items of food because gluttony is a sin and is damaging to the person. It is the excess of wine drinking and the drinking of it for habitual entertainment that God condemns. God condemns heavy drinking (Proverbs 23:20). Drunkenness is a sin that has no acceptance from God. It is a work of the flesh (Galatians 5:21; Isaiah 5:11, 22; Hosea 4:11; 7:5; Joel 1:5; Amos 6:1, 6; Leviticus 10:9; Matthew 24:48-51; Luke 12:45, 46; 1 Corinthians 5:11; 6:10; 11:21; Romans 13:13; Ephesians 5:18; 1 Thessalonians 5:7; 1 Timothy 3:3; 1 Peter 4:3; 2 Peter 2:13).

No wonder God said, "Woe to those who are heroes in drinking wine, and valiant men in mixing strong drink" (Isaiah 5:22), and, "Wine is a mocker, strong drink a brawler, and whoever is intoxicated by it is not wise" (Proverbs 20:1). Drunkenness so affects a person's physical, social, spiritual, and mental make-up that no drunkard can be a part of the kingdom of God (1 Corinthians 6:10).

There is probably no way to know all the problems that drunkenness causes in our modern age. More Americans are killed on the highway by drunk drivers every year than were killed during the entire Korean War or Vietnamese War or World War II. What has the excess of alcohol cost us in infidelity, illegitimate births, neglect of children, welfare, crime, police protection, insurance rates, violence, homicides, family break-ups, bribes, irresponsible decisions at top leadership levels, accidents, health costs, business loss, and inflation? (Work-related losses due to alcohol now total more than eight billion dollars a year, and consumers pay for that.)

Excess of drinking is probably the leading factor behind more moral wrong and more material cost than any other single factor. It is devastating. In the Old Testament, it was the blame for the shame of Noah (Genesis 9:21-24) and the incest of Lot (Genesis 19:30-38); it had a part in murders, poor decisions of kings, and even the downfall of whole kingdoms. No wonder a drunkard son was to be punished by death (Deuteronomy 21:20, 21).

But many today have nearly made drinking to excess a sophisticated way to live. Wine is no longer for food but for fun. It is marketed as the key to success, happiness, and fulfillment. Never do we see the skid row drunks advertising alcohol. Seldom do we see the producers of alcohol warning against the danger of excess. Never do we see that certain kinds of strong drink are not food at all, but damaging drugs that immediately deteriorate the mind and body. Never do we read that just one ounce of alcohol reduces reaction time by 6%. Never do we see "Caution—alcohol destroys brain cells, which are never replaced."

The social pressure to drink is great. It is billed as the acceptable thing to do and the adult thing to do; so we saturate our sporting events on TV with beer advertisements. It is the smart thing to do; so "intellectual" magazines are filled with liquor ads. Since drinking is done primarily as a social activity, the pressure by people who drink is powerful. That's the reason God warned against even associating with heavy drinkers. "Do not be with heavy drinkers of wine . . ." (Proverbs 23:20).

Alcoholism
The liquor that is often used today has a high alcoholic content that was not known in Bible days. Those alcoholic beverages that have a highly concentrated alcoholic content hardly qualify as the "wine" of the Bible. In fact, much of the contemporary liquor products qualify more as drugs, and are very addictive. Thus, alcoholism is on the increase and is

one of the major health and social problems in the United States. Between six and ten million Americans are now alcoholics. An alcoholic is a person who is so addicted to alcohol that his habit often interferes with his responsibilities and his interpersonal relationships.

Many people have argued about whether or not alcoholism is a sin or a sickness. Drunkenness is sin whether it is occasional or habitual. However, habitual drunkenness can lead to sickness. Thus, alcoholism can begin in sin and end in both sin and sickness. It is a sickness when the body is physically addicted. But it is also a sin because the person is morally responsible for his condition and can determine to take responsible action to get out of his condition. Treatment for an alcoholic always involves responsible action on the part of the drinker. The prayer of the alcoholic includes his own personal commitment, "God grant me the serenity to accept the things I cannot change, the courage to change the things I can, and the wisdom to know the difference."

Alcoholics do not have to drink. They can change their practices. But they need help. Here is some of the help they need: (1) Realization that drunkenness is wrong, (2) knowledge that change is possible, (3) a desire to change, (4) a supportive group of people who will help him (That's the *koinonia* fellowship we read so much about in the New Testament.), (5) belief in a power bigger than self (That's God.), (6) confession and repentance of the wrongs of drunkenness, (7) prayer, and (8) commitment to change. The conversion of an alcoholic is beautiful to watch.

Every church should encourage alcoholics to be converted. Not just by fire and brimstone preaching, but also by caring, forgiving people who reach out with hope and support—and whose message makes the power of the Holy Spirit and the presence of God's community available. Alcoholics need encouragement, not weekly sermons that only make them feel guilty.

Here are the "twelve steps" of Alcoholics Anonymous that have been very successful in reorienting people to a new way of life:

1. We admitted we were powerless over alcohol—that our lives had become unmanageable.

2. Came to believe that a Power greater than ourselves could restore us to sanity.

3. Made a decision to turn our will and our lives over to the care of God as we understand Him.

4. Made a searching and fearless moral inventory of ourselves.

5. Admitted to God, to ourselves, and to another human being the exact nature of our wrongs.

6. Were entirely ready to have God remove all these defects of character.

7. Humbly asked Him to remove our shortcomings.

8. Made a list of all persons we had harmed, and became willing to make amends to them all.

9. Made direct amends to such people whenever possible, except when to do so would injure them or others.

10. Continued to take personal inventory and when we were wrong promptly admitted it.

11. Sought, through prayer and meditation, to improve our conscious contact with God as we understood Him, praying only for knowledge of His will for us and for the power to carry that out.

12. Having had a spiritual awakening as a result of these steps, we tried to carry this message to alcoholics, and to practice these principles in all our affairs.

What a fantastic commitment. But that personal commitment has been backed with a communication. An alcoholic can call another alcoholic any time of day and receive supportive fellowship when he feels a strong temptation to drink again. His fellow "brother" will come to his presence and stay with him to help keep him from yielding. He doesn't say, "You shouldn't be tempted again. What's the matter with you?"

Is it possible that the church needs to be more of an understanding family who reaches out with presence and care when a fellow member is tempted or yields? Is it possible that we have become so judgmental and gossipy that no one comes to us admitting weaknesses?

Voluntary Prohibition

While the Bible does not command abstinence, it does give us a powerful principle for voluntary prohibition from drinking. While on the one hand, we are not to judge or condemn each other in regard to food or drink (Colossians 2:16), on the other hand, we are to be willing to heed the words of Paul: "It is good not to eat meat or to drink wine, or to do anything by which your brother stumbles" (Romans 14:21). Paul wrote that at a time when people held different opinions about whether or not they could eat meat or drink wine. Paul wrote against two actions: (1) Condemning another who held a divergent opinion about these matters (Romans 14:1-12); (2) exercising our freedom to the hurt of someone else (Romans 14:13-23).

Peer pressure is strong. Consequently, each of us has a responsibility for conducting ourselves in such a way that we do not lead another person into sin. Drinking wine today can easily do that in two ways. (1) Many people in Christianity believe that one social drink is sin. And if they believe that, then they would sin by taking one drink (Romans 14:23). Although I do not believe the Bible teaches total abstinence, I do not want my understanding to lead someone else into sin. (2) Alcoholism is so common in the United States that the Christian must be very careful that he does not cause a converted alcoholic to get entrapped again. And one drink can do it for a converted alcoholic. That's the reason I think it is unwise for a church to use fermented wine in the Lord's Supper.

The liberty of the strong must never become the stumbling block for the weak. Paul put it this way, "But take care lest this liberty of yours somehow become a stumbling block to the weak" (1 Corinthians 8:9). Although drinking wine is lawful, we must not become mastered by it (1 Corinthians 6:12). In fact, we must be mastered by a desire to be the servant of others, which includes making moral decisions that will help others become and remain reconciled to God (1 Corinthians 9:19-27). That calls for us to be responsible to the people around us in the situation of the moment.

It would be easier for us to have a clear-cut command—"Thou shalt not drink—even one drink." But God didn't give us that command. Instead, he gave us responsibility with liberty. It is far better to teach our children and ourselves the responsibility God has given to us than the abstinence He has not given to us. That sense of responsibility may be God's strongest motivation for us to practice abstinence in the kind of culture in which we live. If so, then it is abstinence wrapped in the package of *agape* love. It's abstinence that squares with the Word of God, not with the precepts of man taught as doctrines of God.

But be careful lest your abstinence become a judgmental bench for condemning another person who does not practice total abstinence. A person's lack of total abstinence may violate your traditions, opinions, and practice, but it may not violate God's command. God does condemn excess, and so must we.

For Your Consideration or Discussion

1 How much does the class know about the philosophy and programs of Alcoholics Anonymous? Read the twelve steps of AA on pages 116, 117 and discuss it, with special reference to the spiritual content of these steps.
2. Discuss the question of why some people are able to drink moderately without abusing alcohol and others are not.
3. How does one know when one is, or is becoming, an alcoholic?
4. Is alcoholism a sin or sickness? Discuss it.
5. Is there a case for abstinence? List all the reasons you can think of which would support a commitment to abstinence.
6. An abstinent person is a stronger Christian than those who drink moderately? Agree_____ Disagree_____ Discuss it.
7. It is widely agreed that Alcoholics Anonymous is the most effective program for treatment of alcoholism in existence. If you are using this book with a class, have an AA member speak to your class on the program of AA. Or have a class member research AA and report.

Chapter 11

AN ETHICAL SMORGASBORD

The list of moral issues that deserve discussing seems endless. Deciding which issues to leave out of a book like this is more difficult than deciding which issues to include. It's somewhat like going to a smorgasbord dinner with a table of food that never ends. While it isn't easy to leave anything off the plate, it is essential. Many times, the only thing to do in order to get a broader sampling is to take small helpings of several items. That's what we will do in this chapter. Each one of the issues in this chapter deserves a fuller treatment. And many other issues not in this book deserve to be in this chapter. But that's the heartache of limitation in space. Recognizing the limitations involved, let's take a look at a few other ethical issues in a smorgasbord fashion.

Drugs

Drug-taking is not a modern idea. Some of the oldest records of civilization speak of certain kinds of drug-taking. The New Testament word *sorcery* referred to drug-taking. The Greek word is *pharmakeia,* from which we get our English word *pharmacy.*

Not all drug-taking is bad. The Greek word *pharmakeia* was first used to describe the medical use of drugs. However, it was early discovered that using drugs too quickly or too often, even for medical purposes, was dangerous. Plato wrote that nondangerous diseases should not be further complicated by the use of drugs.

It is possible that some who condemn the "hard-core" drug addicts are themselves hooked on some kind of drug and do not realize it. It would be interesting to see what is inside the medicine cabinet of every household in the

United States. Some statistics show that Americans take two tons of tranquilizers every day. Is it possible that much of the nation would have a mental breakdown if tranquilizers were outlawed?

The health of a person is a holistic matter relating to his interpersonal relationships, exercise, mental thought patterns, use of his tongue, and more. All of those areas affect the chemical balance inside a person. Consequently, being too quick to prescribe or take some kind of drug may be a way to cover up symptoms instead of getting to root-causes and, thus, to cures.

While the habit of using too many drugs for medical purposes is probably as dysfunctional as it is beneficial, the neglect to use any drugs for medical purposes is also dysfunctional. This is God's creation. He knows us, and He has provided resources in His creation for man's good. We should see those resources as gifts from Him and use them with discretion.

The Greek word *pharmakeia* (sorcery) eventually began to be used to describe the misuse of drugs. Any good thing can be misused. The misuse of drugs poisons rather than cures. It is this misuse of drugs that the Bible condemns under the name of sorcery, which is called a work of the flesh (Galatians 5:20). People are condemned who do not repent from their sorceries (Revelation 9:21). The sorcerers are considered to be as morally perverted as the unbelieving, abominable, murderers, sexual perverts, idolaters, and liars, whose place in eternity will be the lake of fire (Revelation 21:8). The sorcerers are part of that group that will be outside Heaven (Revelation 22:15).

There are several different categories of drugs that are dependency-inducing. They cause a person to become either physically or emotionally dependent upon the drug.

• *Narcotics.* A narcotic is a depressant and a pain-killer. Some of the narcotics are opium, morphine, heroin, codeine, meperidine, methadone, laudanum, and demerol. When taken medically, they must be prescribed by a doctor with the usage closely controlled. Heroin is the popular drug in this category being used by addicts. It is an illegal drug and cannot lawfully be imported or manufactured, but it is a profit-maker for organized crime. Its continual use will kill a person—sometimes suddenly and sometimes gradually with slow pain and physical disorders.

• *Barbiturates.* The barbiturates include sedatives, tranquilizers, and alcohol. Sleeping pills are barbiturates. Many consider barbiturates as the most dangerous category of all, although some have a legitimate medical use. But outside the medical usage, the dangers mount. The abuse of barbiturates can cause a person to slur, stagger, and have temper tantrums and hallucinations. An overdose can kill a person. A person builds a natural tolerance to barbiturates. Consequently, he must continually increase the dosage to get the same effect. Withdrawal often causes death.

• *Hallucinogens.* These are the mind-stretching drugs, which include marijuana, LSD, and DMT. These drugs affect the nervous system and cause the user to "take a trip." The "trip" can include distorted color, sounds, and height/depth concepts. For instance, a person on the twentieth floor may step off the ledge thinking he is stepping off a curb. The world becomes "unreal"—words lose meanings, time seems to stop—so life around the person has no meaning, and the person himself loses his sense of being a real person with worth and meaning.

There is much talk about the harmless use of marijuana. Marijuana affects people differently. That's part of its danger. No one can tell in advance how marijuana will affect him. However, marijuana does intoxicate a person and can cause him to distort reality, for it is an hallucinogen. While marijuana does not seem to cause physical dependence, it may cause mental dependence, which can become even more dangerous to a person.

• *Amphetamines* are stimulant drugs. The most widely used in the United States is caffein, which is found in coffee, tea, and cola drinks. Cocaine and the pep pills are also amphetamines. Pills to stay awake while studying or driving are amphetamines. The abuse of these drugs can lead a person to become irritable and violent.

The misuse of drugs in Jesus' day became connected with trying to handle life in some kind of magical way. Consequently, drug taking was eventually connected with witchcraft and astrology.

One of the primary dangers of the abuse of drugs today relates directly to trying to handle life in some kind of "magical" power that leaves God out. Life is not lived well by an intake of drugs, but by a personal, responsive, obedient relationship with God, His Son, and His Spirit. It is not possible to be dependent both upon drugs and God. One or the other must go.

Occultism

While this may sound like an out-of-place topic in a book on ethics, it really isn't. Occultism has become the way of life for some people. It has both directed their ethics and become their ethics. One of the reasons God condemned occultism is because of what it leads people to do ethically. Here are some of the occult practices condemned in the Bible:

• *Astrology.* The idea that life is controlled by the position of the stars is centuries old. The idea grew out of observations, record keeping, and false conclusions. Astrologers observed the movements of heavens while others observed what happened at the same time on earth. The false conclusion arose that whatever happened on earth is determined by what happens among the heavenly bodies. It is true that *some* things on earth do correspond to what happens among the heavenly bodies. For instance, the moon affects the tide. The sun affects the heat. The movement of the sun affects the seasons. However, *some* of that is really the movement of the earth, not the stars.

From a detailed study of the heavenly bodies, twelve zodiacs were defined. This is the basis for the horoscope in the newspapers today. The whole system is based on error. First of all, we have discovered more about the heavenly bodies than the system was based upon. Secondly, man does not live by fatalism, but by faith. Our life isn't *determined* by the stars at all. To do that is to make the heavenly bodies divine. God condemns that (Amos 5:26, 27; Acts 7:43). Paul spoke against that when he used terms astrologers used in one of his most popular passages:

For I am convinced that neither death, nor life, nor angels, nor principalities, nor things present, nor things to come, nor powers, nor height, nor depth, nor any other created thing, shall be able to separate us from the love of God, which is in Christ Jesus our Lord (Romans 8:38, 39).

"Things present and things to come" and "height and depth" were astrologer's terms to talk about where the stars are located, where they are going, and how high or low they are located. Paul was saying none of that makes any difference.

• *Divination.* This is the practice of depending upon some material means to get a message from God. It includes looking into a crystal ball, consulting the dead in seances, using a *Ouija* board, using witchcraft, and using a medium to contact the spirits. God condemns all of that (Deuteronomy 18:10, 11; 2 Kings 21:6). It is true that Saul did that, but his action was condemned (1 Chronicles 10:13). Those who use the occult way to decide how to live by-pass the source God himself has given to us—the Bible (2 Timothy 3:16, 17).

Neutral Choices

"Oh we got trouble! Right here in River City! Trouble with a capital T, and that rhymes with P and that stands for pool!"*

When I was a boy, playing pool was sin. But is it really? Is knocking a ball into a hole on a green table sin, while knocking a ball into a hole on green grass is not sin? Is playing pool moral, immoral, or amoral? Some things are moral regardless of what people say about them. For instance, faithfulness to one's mate is the right way to live regardless of how many people vote against it. When God says something is right, it is right. Some things are immoral regardless of how many people say it is the "O.K." thing to do. When God calls something wrong, it is wrong.

But most of our daily ethical decisions fall under the category of the amoral. The amoral issues are the neutral issues. They are neither moral nor immoral in and of themselves, but they can become either moral or immoral. Unless we have a clear word from God that a practice is sin, it is probably a neutral practice.

*Meredith Willson, *The Music Man* (New York: G. P. Putnam's Sons)

The list of the neutral areas is nearly endless. It includes such things as playing pool (or golf), playing cards (or *Monopoly*), dancing, going to a movie (or theater), watching television, and eating certain kinds of food.

The problem with any neutral ethical practice is that any one of these *could* be a sin for *some* people while not a sin for other people. In the neutral areas, we do not have an absolute right or wrong. What's right for one may be wrong for another. If a person *thinks* a practice is a sin and does it with that understanding, his action is a sinful action. Although the act is neutral, his attitude of rebellion is not neutral. That's what Paul was saying when he said, "But he who doubts is condemned if he eats, because his eating is not from faith; and whatever is not from faith is sin" (Romans 14:23).

In that day, some Christians thought it was sin to eat pork and other foods. Others did not think so. Those who thought it was sin based their belief upon God's Word in Leviticus 11. God later lifted that ban (Mark 7:18, 19; Acts 10:9-15; Colossians 2:16). However, some Christians either did not know about that or were allowing the way they were reared to continue to affect their evaluation of eating pork. (Surely we can relate to that. A person today who is reared from infancy believing that going to any movie is sin will have a difficult time growing out of that belief.)

One of the main difficulties Paul had to face was how Christians with different understandings about the neutral areas looked upon each other and treated each other and conducted themselves in those neutral areas when in each other's presence.

Sometimes Christians condemned other Christians who engaged in those neutral areas. To that situation, Paul wrote the following:

> Therefore let no one act as your judge in regard to food or drink or in respect to a festival or a new moon or a Sabbath day—things which are a mere shadow of what is to come; but the substance belongs to Christ (Colossians 2:16, 17).

> Now accept the one who is weak in faith, but not for the purpose of passing judgment on his opinions. One man has faith that he may eat all things, but he who is weak eats vegetables only. Let not him who eats regard with contempt him who does

not eat, and let not him who does not eat judge him who eats, for God has accepted him. Who are you to judge the servant of another? To his own master he stands or falls; and stand he will, for the Lord is able to make him stand (Romans 14:1-4).

Therefore let us not judge one another any more, but rather determine this—not to put an obstacle or a stumbling block in a brother's way (Romans 14:13).

Sometimes Christians thought, "Okay, if another can do it, I can do it, even though I still believe it is wrong." To that Paul wrote:

I know and am convinced in the Lord Jesus that nothing is unclean in itself; but to him who thinks anything to be unclean, to him it is unclean (Romans 14:14).

Sometimes Christians were not sensitive to how other Christians felt; so they engaged in certain neutral areas, knowing it would offend a brother or sister. To that situation Paul wrote:

For if because of food your brother is hurt, you are no longer walking according to love. Do not destroy with your food him for whom Christ died. Therefore do not let what is for you a good thing be spoken of as evil; for the kingdom of God is not eating and drinking, but righteousness and peace and joy in the Holy Spirit (Romans 14:15-17).

Do not tear down the work of God for the sake of food. All things indeed are clean, but they are evil for the man who eats and gives offense. It is good not to eat meat or to drink wine, or to do anything by which your brother stumbles (Romans 14:20, 21).

For if someone sees you, who have knowledge, dining in an idol's temple, will not his conscience, if he is weak, be strengthened to eat things sacrificed to idols? For through your knowledge he who is weak is ruined, the brother for whose sake Christ died. And thus, by sinning against the brethren and wounding their conscience when it is weak, you sin against Christ. Therefore, if food causes my brother to stumble, I will never eat meat again, that I might not cause my brother to stumble (1 Corinthians 8:10-13).

But just what did Paul mean by "giving offense" or "hurting" a brother who sees you doing a neutral practice? He was not speaking about upsetting him. No one upset more people by His practices than Jesus. Jesus upset people by such things as doing some good deeds on the Sabbath and talking with women in public. If we can't do anything that "offends" someone, then we must stop living. Some people can be offended if they see that we have an air-conditioned car. They may sacrifice air conditioning to have more money to send to the mission field, and so they think all others should do the same. Some people can be offended by seeing us order a "deluxe hamburger" instead of a regular hamburger, for the deluxe costs more. Some people can be offended if a man wears a white shirt or cowboy boots, or has hair that touches his ears or has a flat-top. Living in a way that no one is offended is impossible. In fact, to attempt that kind of living will cause a person to put aside all of his commitments. Jesus offended many people—yet He did not sin.

When Paul talked about backing off of doing neutral moral practices when they would offend people, he was not talking about "offense" in the popular way we use the word today. The Greek word for offense really means stumbling block. It was a word used to describe something that tripped someone like a rock that protrudes from the ground. While all neutral issues are lawful, some can be the "rocks" that cause another to fall into sin, and Christians need to be sensitive to that when they know that another Christian in his presence considers a neutral area as sin *and* our practice of it in his presence would cause him to practice it. So Paul was speaking about our willingness to refrain from a practice which we *know* is not sin, but which we also *know* someone else thinks is sin *and we know our doing it would motivate him to do it.* Jesus did many things that the Pharisees thought were sin. And Jesus did those things in their presence. But He knew that His action would not motivate them to do the acts also. However, when we *know* that our action would motivate another to do the same action that he thinks is sin, then we have caused our brother to stumble.

Although *we* have the liberty to do the neutral areas without sin, we must not misuse that liberty in a way that motivates another to sin. That's what Paul was communicating when he said:

For though I am free from all men, I have made myself a slave to all, that I might win the more. And to the Jews I became as a Jew, that I might win Jews; to those who are under the Law, as under the Law, though not being myself under the Law, that I might win those who are under the Law; to those who are without law, as without law, though not being without the law of God but under the law of Christ, that I might win those who are without law. To the weak I became weak, that I might win the weak; I have become all things to all men, that I may by all means save some. And I do all things for the sake of the gospel, that I may become a fellow-partaker of it (1 Corinthians 9:19-23).

To live like that with the neutral issues is to enjoy our liberty while at the same time loving our brother.

For Your Consideration or Discussion

1. Project: Discuss with a medical doctor or pharmacist the various drugs—their use and limits.
2. Discuss Martin Luther's statement: "A Christian is a perfectly free lord of all, subject to none. A Christian is a perfectly dutiful servant of all, subject to all." Apply this statement to the question of whether the Christian is free to drink wine or engage in other "ethically neutral" activities.
3. Project: If you are studying this book as part of a class, have a capable class member research and report on the occult. If you are fortunate enough to have a Christian in your area who is an authority on the occult, arrange to have that person speak to your class.

Chapter 12

ONCE IN SIN ALWAYS IN SIN?

Dear Down:

Just recently several of those in positions of Christian leadership in our area have been distressed by evident deficiencies in the ethical conduct of a few of those sharing these activities with them. Definite cases of severe moral turpitude have surfaced leading to great embarrassment and confusion in the larger Christian community to which these persons belong. One is torn between the desire not to be "judgmental" and fear of being so seemingly oblivious to such acts that one will leave the impression that "it makes no difference."

Of course, Down, such acts hurt. They hurt the ones who do them, their loved ones, friends, associates, and the church at large. Yet let me just present a hypothetical case to you. Just suppose there is an outstanding religious figure who has risen from humble origins in a rural setting to a place of relative prestige and power. His influence and his work for God have been wholesome and helpful. His words are cherished and quoted by many. Suddenly it becomes known to several that he has committed adultery and has engaged in underhanded and most harmful—even fatal—efforts to "cover up" this indiscretion. Now he says he repents and wants to continue to be accepted as a leader among the people of God. What should our attitude be?

Several things should be kept in mind. Does this serious lapse from righteousness make invalid all the good and useful things he has done, said, and written before this happened? Does the recognition of this failure preclude any future good influence for God? Most would say the answer to the first is, "Generally, no," and to the second, "No, if there is sincere repentance and if subsequent conduct proves the validity of that repentance."

The case presented, of course, is a real one—that of David. That he was guilty of adultery and conspiracy to commit murder did not mean the Twenty-third Psalm was not of enduring spiritual value. His earnest repentance, as evidenced in Psalm 51, and his later actions, showed he did return to the Lord and "brought forth fruits meet for repentance."

As Bishop Joseph Hall writes of David's sins in his *Contemplations*, "O thou royal Prophet and Prophetical King of Israel, where shall I find ought to extenuate that crime for which God himself hath noted thee? . . . Who can promise himself always to stand, when he sees thee fallen, and maimed with the fall?"

Such an example, Down, should keep us from supercilious self-assurance on the one hand, and, if there is failure on our part or on the part of others, from judgmental severity or from unrelieved despair.

Balancingly your,

*Thistle**

When Jesus said, "Any sin and blasphemy shall be forgiven men, but blasphemy against the Spirit" (Matthew 12:31), that's precisely what He meant—any sin: incest, murder, adultery, abortion—ANY sin. Name it, and it is forgiveable. And it's forgiveable for ANYONE.

I could not be in the church, in ministry, and writing this book were it not for the forgiveness of God. I have sinned against God—not only prior to becoming a Christian, but also afterwards. But God is in the forgiving business. That's one of His specialties. God does not lock us up into our past sins. He frees us from those to a future of usefulness. Forgiveness is the gift of God offered to us in Jesus (Ephesians 1:7).

But forgiveness that comes *from* God is to come *through* people. I could not be in the church, in ministry, and writing this book were it not for the forgiveness of others. I have sinned against others. Some of my sins have been so serious against others that all earthly relationships with them should have been severed permanently. But God has intervened. He has not only reconciled us to himself, but also given to us the ministry of reconciliation (2 Corinthians 5:18). When Paul wrote that "God was in Christ reconciling the world to Himself, not counting their trespasses against them, and He has committed to us the word of reconciliation" (2 Corinthians 5:19), he was saying that as God was in Christ, so

*Thistle, "Just Suppose," *Christian Standard*, Vol. 116, No. 51, December 20, 1981, p. 7.

God is in us (Ephesians 2:22), so that we do not count people's trespasses against them, but we give them the word of reconciliation—"I forgive"—as Jesus did. Paul made that clear when he wrote that we are to be "forgiving each other, just as God in Christ also has forgiven you" (Ephesians 4:32). There is little place and value within the family of God unless members will forgive each other. The only other alternative is to carry grudges to destroy one another. Without forgiveness, there can be no unity within God's family. Forgiving others is not an option, but a mandate for the Christian. Jesus said, "For if you forgive men their transgressions, your heavenly Father will also forgive you. But if you do not forgive men, then your Father will not forgive your transgressions" (Matthew 6:14, 15). That is true for many reasons. Here are a few of them:

● (1) Forgiving others communicates God's character and plan. Failure to forgive others negates what God wants for sinners.

● (2) Forgiving others gives to people an objective demonstration that forgiveness is really possible. Forgiveness from God is difficult to believe if people do not experience it from God's people. God's forgiveness needs human skin wrapped around it. If we "love" people but won't forgive, how can they know that God's love will naturally lead to forgiveness?

● (3) Forgiveness gives to the forgiver a peace of mind that God wants for us. It was after Paul wrote, "Bearing with one another, and forgiving each other, whoever has a complaint against anyone; just as the Lord forgave you, so also should you," that he wrote, "And let the peace of Christ rule in your hearts, to which indeed you were called in one body; and be thankful" (Colossians 3:13, 15). Forgiveness is essential for peace to rule, unity to be present (one body), and thankfulness to exist. Nothing clears away the poisonous smog or interpersonal animosities but forgiveness.

● (4) Forgiving the person who has sinned against us demonstrates that we have received God's forgiveness of our sins against Him. The person who really believes and accepts God's forgiveness also offers that to others (Matthew 18:33). Failure to forgive others invites condemnation to self (Matthew 18:34, 35). Only if you have never needed or will never need forgiveness do you dare consider refusing to forgive another. Once General James Oglethorpe said to John Wesley, "I will never forgive." John Wesley replied, "Then I hope, sir, that you never sin!" George Herbert once wrote, "He that cannot forgive others breaks the bridge over which he himself must pass if he would ever reach heaven; for everyone has need to be forgiven."

The person who does not forgive another either *cannot* because he does not have God's Spirit, or *will not* because he doesn't have God's humility and love.

But how often should we forgive another? On one occasion, Peter tried to make himself look good when he suggested seven times (Matthew 18:21). Surely seven times is enough, if not too much. But Jesus, in essence, replied, "Where did you ever come up with that figure, Peter? You did not learn that one from me. Haven't you noticed how many times people have hurt me? Did I stop forgiving after seven times? If you want a figure—how about this one—'seventy times seven' " (Matthew 18:22).

What? Who can keep track of that many times? But that's Jesus' point—don't be keeping score. Love "keeps no record of wrongs" (1 Corinthians 13:5, NIV).

Jesus then told a parable (Matthew 18:23-35) to illustrate that our forgiveness to another ought to be as big as a person's sin against us. He told about a person who forgave one of his servants of a debt of ten thousand talents (that's an incredible amount—equal to 60 million days' pay). But the servant who was forgiven got the big head. He thought he was so deserving of his forgiveness that he failed to identify with another person who needed forgiveness. He had evidently forgotten the hurt that he had gone through before his forgiveness. He had evidently forgotten that his life was totally at the mercy of his master. He had forgotten that he was a nobody who was ready to throw in the towel until he was forgiven. He had evidently forgotten that he had no future, no hope, no peace, without the forgiveness of another. So he refused to forgive another person who owed him a measly one hundred days' pay. When that happened, the lord became angry and said, "You wicked slave, I forgave you all that debt because you entreated me. Should you not also have had mercy on your fellow slave, even as I had mercy on you?"

It is clear that we receive forgiveness from God not for the purpose of bottling it up inside us to forget we are sinners, but partly for the purpose of passing forgiveness on to others. And if we don't, it's a sign we have not appreciated His forgiveness and used it properly. So the lord handed that unforgiving person over to the torturer. The lord caused that man to eat his own bitter medicine. Then Jesus said, "So shall my heavenly Father also do to you, if each of you does not forgive his brother from your heart."

The person who knows what it means to need forgiveness and receives it becomes a broken person who is humbled enough to forgive others. Until our hearts are broken down by sin, and until we find ourselves crying out to God for forgiveness, we hang on too much to our own egos. We inwardly believe that God saves us because we really deserve it. We think we are pretty good folks and do a lot for God, so we deserve salvation. When we think like that, we find it hard to forgive others when they fall. We think we are better than they are; after all, they should have known better than to make that mistake.

Only when we truly sense the need for forgiveness, when we truly sense our own faults and weaknesses, do we realize that we are on the level of everyone else—that we are simply beggars, made poor by sin, in need of God's forgiveness and salvation. It is then that we can extend forgiveness to others and mean it.

God promised to judge us by the same standard we use to judge others. Jesus said, "For in the same way you judge, you will be judged, and with the measure you use, it will be measured to you" (Matthew 7:2, NIV). James declared, "Judgment will be merciless to one who has shown no mercy; mercy triumphs over judgment" (James 2:13). Do we exercise grace or retaliation? Mercy or harshness? Forgetfulness or remembering? Reconciliation or animosity?

A major tragedy in the church occurs when one member will not forgive another. It may be true that the initial sin caused disharmony and hurt, but the unforgiving reaction may be a bigger sin in that it perpetuates the disharmony and hurt. The ministry of reconciliation should be demonstrated best within the church. If we cannot be united with brothers and sisters who have sinned against us, how can we possibly be united with barbarians who sin against us? We must

> get rid of all bitterness, rage and anger, brawling and slander, along with every form of malice. Be kind and compassionate to one another, forgiving each other, just as in Christ God forgave you. Be imitators of God, therefore, as dearly beloved children and live a life of love, just as Christ loved us and gave himself up for us . . . (Ephesians 4:31—5:2, NIV).

If a brother sins, we should restore him gently (Galatians 6:1, see also James 5:19, 20), even if he has sinned against us (Matthew 5:23, 24; 6:12; 18:15-35).

It is easy to talk about forgiveness until we ourselves get hurt. I am convinced that forgiveness is the toughest sacrifice a person makes. It denies the self that loves to demand its "rights." Forgiveness is the willingness to accept undeserved suffering. When we forgive another person, we voluntarily accept the hurt he has hurled at us. When we forgive, we actually bear the penalty of that other person's sin against us. That's the reason forgiveness is one of the most Christlike things we can do. It is the highest expression of unselfishness. It is the grandest demonstration of dying to self and rising to a newness of life. The cost is high, but the value of it is much higher than the cost.

Real forgiveness must be coupled with restored fellowship. It is one thing to say, "I'll forgive, but I will never respect that person again and never want to see him again." That is not the forgiveness that Christ offers us. We are to "accept one another, then, just as Christ accepted you" (Romans 15:7, NIV). Real forgiveness is seen when the person who has been hurt goes out of his way to serve the needs of the one who has sinned against him. That is what God and Christ have done for us. Paul said, "Brethren, even if a man is caught in any trespass, you who are spiritual, restore such a one in a spirit of gentleness; each one looking to yourself, lest you too be tempted" (Galatians 6:1).

Forgiving calls for compassion. So often when someone sins against us, we say, "I don't understand him." We don't have to understand him, but we do need to be understanding. We need to know that the other person is hurting and needs healing. Paul wrote, "Bear one another's burdens, and thus fulfill the law of Christ" (Galatians 6:2). Our goal is not to understand all, for there is much that's going on in another person's life. However, we are to be understanding in all.

The Bible is filled with people who became fruitful partly because they forgave others. Sarah forgave Abraham for allowing her to be taken into a king's harem. Esau forgave Jacob for taking the birthright and the blessing of his father away from him. At one time, he declared he wanted to kill Jacob. But the next time they met, he held no grudge and would take no gift to patch things up. He said, "I already have plenty, my brother. . . . Let us be on our way; I'll accompany you" (Genesis 33:9-12, NIV).

Joseph forgave his brothers for hating him, making fun of him, and selling him. In fact, when he saw them, he wept and saved their lives. Joseph named his two sons after the characteristics that dominated his life and contributed to his success: "God has made me *forget* all my trouble" (Manasseh) and "God has made me *fruitful*" (Ephraim, Genesis 41:51, 52). There is a direct relationship between being able to forget the hurts that have been perpetrated against us and being fruitful in our lives.

Forgiving is not easy, but it is essential. It should be practiced, first of all, in our homes. More marriages would continue through not only "the better" but also through "the worse" if husbands and wives would forgive each other. More homes would be refuges if parents would forgive children and children would forgive parents.

Forgiveness must also extend to those outside the church. We are just kidding ourselves if we claim we can "forgive" those outsiders who have never hurt us when we won't forgive the "insiders" who have. The privilege of living in Heaven among people who have sinned on earth will be partly determined by our willingness to forgive them—in the here and now.

There are certain valuable steps that are necessary for restoration of the broken relationships that sin causes. The first step is to confront a person with his sin. Sin is so deceiving. It blinds us to the truth—even though we may have every verse about sin memorized. The "god" of this world is crafty and knows how to desensitize us to sin. Consequently, it becomes a merciful act to go to the sinner and show him his fault just between the two of you (Matthew 18:15). Keeping it private is important. Sin always hurts people. It is unkind to hurt others by exposing sin publicly. If the sinner listens, that is as far as the knowledge about the sin has to go.

If he does listen and repent, the person sinned against has the responsibility to extend forgiveness. The church at Corinth did not understand that. They refused to forgive a brother who had sinned (2 Corinthians 2:6-11). Thus, Paul reminded them that God is the "Father of mercies and God of all comfort" (1:3) and that God comforts "so that we may be able to comfort those who are in any affliction . . ." (1:4).

The second step toward forgiveness is to let a person know that we forgive him. Telling him of that forgiveness is as important as forgiving him. If you don't, the distance between you will never be closed. While your mind may be clear and you hold no animosity within your heart, when the person sees you, he will never know that unless you tell him. He will always wonder what you are thinking about him. He needs to know of your forgiveness in order to feel it.

Forgiveness is still not complete with these two steps. The next step is, as Paul says, to "comfort him" (2 Corinthians 2:7). The Greek word for comfort literally means "to stand alongside of." The idea is to be an encourager of that person, to be a "stand-by" to him rather than a bystander. This is how brothers and sisters in a human family should treat each other in spite of hurts if there is to be unity in that human family. It should also be the life-style within the family of God. Without this comforting step, the brother who sinned may be "overwhelmed by excessive sorrow" (2 Corinthians 2:7).

There is yet another step—"reaffirm your love to him" (2 Corinthians 2:8). The word "love" (agape) stresses unselfish outreach for the other person's benefit. It involves doing for the other person what he needs. That is super tough, but that is the way toward reconciliation. Jesus expressed that type of love for every one of His disciples who denied Him. In fact, some of the appearances during forty days after His resurrection were designed to reaffirm His love for them.

Parents do that with erring children, and Christians are to do that for each other.

While the person who has been sinned against has some responsibilities, so does the person who sinned. He is to (1) admit his sin; (2) take responsibility for it; (3) regret the hurt it has caused; (4) turn from that sin completely.

But even that is not all. He should be so humbled by that other person's forgiveness that he thanks God for the forgiveness regularly. He should be willing to serve that other person's well being. He should love that person with that *agape* unselfish outreach for that person's benefit.

He should not receive the forgiveness so lightly that he brushes off the seriousness of his sin. Although David received forgiveness, he still wrote, "For I know my transgressions, and my sin is ever before me" (Psalm 51:3). That awareness did not weigh David down so he could not serve God or man. But it did keep David humble as one who was permitted to serve because he had been forgiven. David knew that what he was able to do for God was not *because* of David, but *in spite of* David. And so David lived with the awareness that he was fallible and so prayed, "Create in me a clean heart, O God, and renew a steadfast spirit within me" (Psalm 51:10).

Sin surely breaks our pride, and the forgiveness of others surely breaks down our sense of self-sufficiency. We do need one another. And the more our environment is filled with sin all around us, the more we need each other. That's what it means to be a family—a family of God.

I cannot make it as a Christian without the support that others have poured into my life. Part of that support has come from those who humbly obeyed the will of God who admonishes us to forgive each other (Colossians 3:13).

Only because of forgiveness do we have contributions from Noah, who got drunk; Abraham, who pawned off his wife; Lot, who committed incest while drunk; Moses, who murdered; Jacob, who cheated and committed polygamy; Judah, who had an affair with his daughter-in-law and begat two of his grandsons; Samson, who had temper tantrums and sexual affairs; Jepthah, who was an illegitimate runaway who ran with a gang and raided at night; David, who was a peeping tom, adulterer, and schemer of murder; Rahab, who was a prostitute; and Paul, who was the "Hitler" of the first century, masterminding his own holocaust. The list goes on. And on that list am I.

Sin does not have to be the last word when we violate any of the ethical issues we have looked at in this book. "Once in sin always in sin" does not have to be. God is a liberator. And He has called us to be His partner in liberating others.

Praise God for forgiveness!!

For Your Consideration or Discussion

1. Is apologizing equal to repentance, and is verbal acceptance of the apology the same as forgiveness?
2. Is it possible that saying, "I forgive you," is an act of arrogance and pride rather than humility and love? Does "I forgive you" imply that the other person is totally in the wrong and that we (human beings) are the dispensers of forgiveness rather than God? Should the forgiving person also apologize—always? sometimes? never?
3. Who should take the initiative in forgiving, the "offender" or the "offended"?
4. Are there certain broken relationships where forgiveness is possible but reconciliation (living or working together in harmony) is impossible? Are forgiveness and reconciliation the same?
5. Would you agree that you will not know whether you are a forgiving person until you are called upon to forgive a serious mistreatment of yourself or someone you love?

Chapter 13

HEALING THE LAND

The ethics of a country can never rise above the religion in that country. It never has and never will. God's people can transform a nation. The Messiah's people can lift the moral practices in a community. How do we know that? History proves it. The greatest social changes for the good in this country have always come after major spiritual revivals. (Timothy Smith has objectively substantiated that in his book *Revivalism and Social Reform*, Magnolia, MTA: Peter Smith, Publisher, 1980). For instance, the Great Awakening literally changed the social fiber of this country.

Not only does history prove that God's people are the change-agent variable that alters a national environment, but God also taught it. He indirectly taught it when He promised to spare Sodom if only ten of God's people lived there. Only ten of God's people can make a significant difference in any community. He promised it directly in 2 Chronicles 7:14: "If my people, who are called by my name, will humble themselves and pray and seek my face and turn from their wicked ways, then will I hear from heaven and will forgive their sin and will heal their land" (NIV).

Although those promises were beamed to the people of Israel about the nation of Israel, the principles are valid for any nation in moral trouble. In the one verse are three key elements—promises, people, and practices.

Promises

God made three exciting promises:

• *I will hear from heaven.* "I will hear" tells us many things about God: (1) He is alive. Dead people hear nothing. (2) He yearns to have us communicate with Him. How would you like it if your children communicatively cut themselves off from you? Would you handle it well if they would not talk with you unless they were wanting something from you? God wants to hear us talk with Him. (3) What we say makes a difference. The apostles saw that Jesus' prayer made a difference. They never asked Him to teach them to do miracles, speak in tongues, or teach with effectiveness. But they did ask Him to teach them to pray.

"From heaven" tells us that God is still on His throne. No matter how bad things get, no one has moved God off His throne, and no one will. He is in control and always will be. When John was taken to Heaven, the first thing he saw was a throne—and it wasn't empty. God was on it (Revelation 4:2).

• *And will forgive their sin.* What a glorious promise. For when God forgives, He forgets (Isaiah 65:17; Jeremiah 31:34; Hebrews 8:12; 10:17). It will be impossible to make God remember sins that He has forgiven. You may remember them, and the people against whom you sinned may remember them, but not God. Isn't that a fantastic promise?

At one time I believed that when Jesus returned, I would run to the rocks and hills and ask them to fall on me—even as a Christian. But that's not true. Because God forgets what He forgives. "When He appears, we may have confidence and not shrink away from Him in shame at His coming" (1 John 2:28).

• *And will heal their land.* Since 1972, we have murdered over eleven million unborn children. That's nearly twice the number murdered in Hitler's holocaust. Our land needs healing! Some estimate that one out of every ten Americans is a homosexual. Our land needs healing! Pornography is a billion-dollar business. Our land needs healing! In some places, divorces outnumber marriages. Our land needs healing! Incest is increasingly being seen as a permissible life-style. Our land needs healing! Last year the number-one reason children died was not childhood diseases or accidents, but child abuse. Our land needs healing! Last year the number-two reason teenagers died was suicide. Our land needs healing!

I realize that those statements cast a shadow across our land. But the good news is that it is impossible for a shadow to exist unless the sun is shining at the same time. And the sun is shining. That sun is God's Son, who has risen and lives in His people. Only He who lives in us is greater than He who lives in the world (1 John 4:4), and whoever "is born of God overcomes the world; and this is the victory that has overcome the world—our faith" (1 John 5:4). Despite the moral disease in a country, God promises healing.

But healing is not automatic. God will allow us to be drawn into the cesspool of our immoral garbage if we choose. Be healed in righteousness or be heaped in rubbish—it's our choice. At least twenty-two different civilizations have chosen the latter and have become nonexistent after flourishing as distinct civilizations.

Either we destroy sin, or sin will destroy us. Healing depends upon the right people committed to the right practices.

The Right People and Practices

- *If my people, who are called by my name.* There are those who claim that they are owned by God and live like it. In fact, they get their identity so much from Him that they are called by His name.

God's people make the difference in a nation. That's why God calls His people light, leaven, and salt. Light dispels darkness. Christians have often thought too little of ourselves as a people. Light is power. It is impossible for darkness to eliminate light. All darkness can do is make the light appear brighter. Light exists in order to penetrate and choke back darkness.

Leaven permeates. It is a change agent. The environment does not change the yeast. The yeast does the changing. It brings the environment in which it is placed to a new height.

Salt preserves food by preventing decay. While light changes the dark into the light and leaven further changes, salt is applied to what is already good to keep it from rotting. Christians need to salt each other so we do not become sick as we touch an infested world.

Perhaps God's people have been blaming everyone else for the woes in the country. One man put it this way, "When things go wrong in the nation, I blame the Senate and House. And then if nothing improves, I come home and blame my spouse." It's time for God's people to quit projecting blame on everyone else while passively being happy that we've got correct doctrine nailed down.

God's healing of a nation is conditioned upon a big "if." That "if" not only points to the right people, but also the right practices.

- *Will humble themselves.* That simply means that we do not think we are more important than others because of who we are, where we live, what education we have, or what status we've attained. It means that we do not look out for only our own personal interests, but also the interests of others. It means that we crawl outside our own egos and put on the robe of servanthood to others.

- *And pray.* That simply means that we talk with God. How often do you *really* pray to God other than when you are asking for something for yourself.

- *And seek my face.* That means that we seek His presence. He really wants himself to be a part of what we are doing. We do not say, "Buzz off, God." To seek His face is to want His attitudes, actions, and reactions to become ours.

It is not possible to seek God's presence and purposely by-pass reading the Bible. How often do you really read His word?

- *And turn from their wicked ways.* Let's face it, each of us has some turning to do. The person who doesn't think he has any changes to make to become more Christ-like is a person who thinks He's infallible. The person who thinks he is infallible will become God's competitor instead of God's companion. Turning from wicked ways involves *recognizing* our sin, taking *responsibility* for it without blaming others, *regretting* the hurt it has caused God and others, *resolving* not to do that sin again, and *reforming* from the actual practice.

In 1959, 1/50 of an ounce of plutonium escaped from a nuclear plant in Oak Ridge, Tennessee. But power had escaped, and because of that, changes took place. People within four acres turned in their clothes. The roofs on the building and surrounding buildings were scraped off and replaced. Those buildings were sandblasted and repainted. The asphalt was dug up and hauled off—all because 1/50 of an ounce of some power escaped.

But if God's people would do God's practices, we could make 1/50 ounce of plutonium look like a fizzled firecracker. Some might respond by saying, "That's too simple. A land won't be healed just because God's people do those practices." But the only way we can think like that is if we do not believe God's promises. God is consistently trustworthy to His promises.

I have a dream. I suspect you have a dream. This land—this whole land—can be healed—if!

If my people, who are called by my name, will humble themselves and pray and seek my face and turn from their wicked ways, then will I hear from heaven and will forgive their sin and will heal their land (2 Chronicles 7:14, NIV).

For Your Consideration or Discussion

1. Mr. Staton declares: "The ethics of a country can never rise above the religion in that country." Was there ever a time when the religion of the country was below the ethics of the country ("ethics of the country" is here defined as the moral principles stated in the U.S. Constitution and Bill of Rights)?
2. We sometimes hear the phrase "national pride." On the basis of this book and on the basis of 2 Chronicles 7:14, would it be more appropriate to speak of national humility? Agree or disagree?
3. Suggestion: At the close of this study, make a commitment to pray for the next several months that God would heal the land of America. If you have been involved in a group study, pair into prayer partners or commit yourselves to praying all together. You might pick a certain time each day when all the members will pray, whether or not you meet together.

CHECK THESE BOOKS
by Knofel Staton

Check Your Lifestyle. Step-by-step Guidelines on how to make the principles of Proverbs come to life in the 20th century. A practical book that moves Christianity into the "nitty-gritty of daily living.

Check Your Character. A soul-searching study of the Beatitudes—"the beautiful attitudes of Jesus'—in the Sermon on the Mount. The Beautitudes explain Jesus'sometimes perplexing behavior—and the rightness of the same behavior for us today.

Check Your Discipleship. A penetrating look at the lives of Jesus and His disciples, with practical application to make our own lives like theirs.

Check Your Homelife. A practical guide to make life around your house more peaceful, more loving, and more Christ-like.

Check Your Life in Christ. A probing study of what it means to be "in Christ." This book provides answers to the questions Christians ask about their life in Christ.

Available at your Christian bookstore or

STANDARD PUBLISHING